WB JAZZ PIANO LIBRARY

Early Intermediate Piano Solos
Level Three

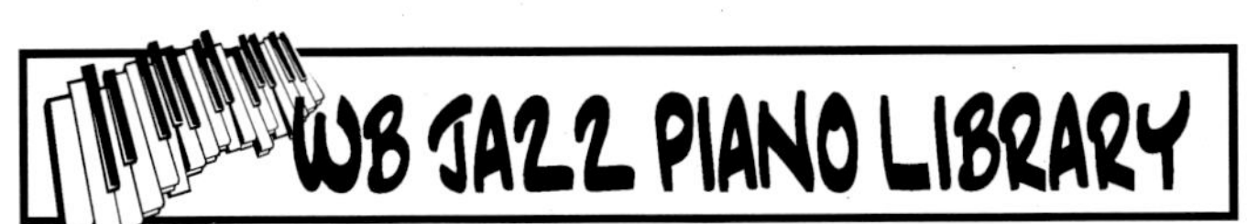

JAZZ MONTAGE

8 Jazz Piano Solos

by LARRY MINSKY

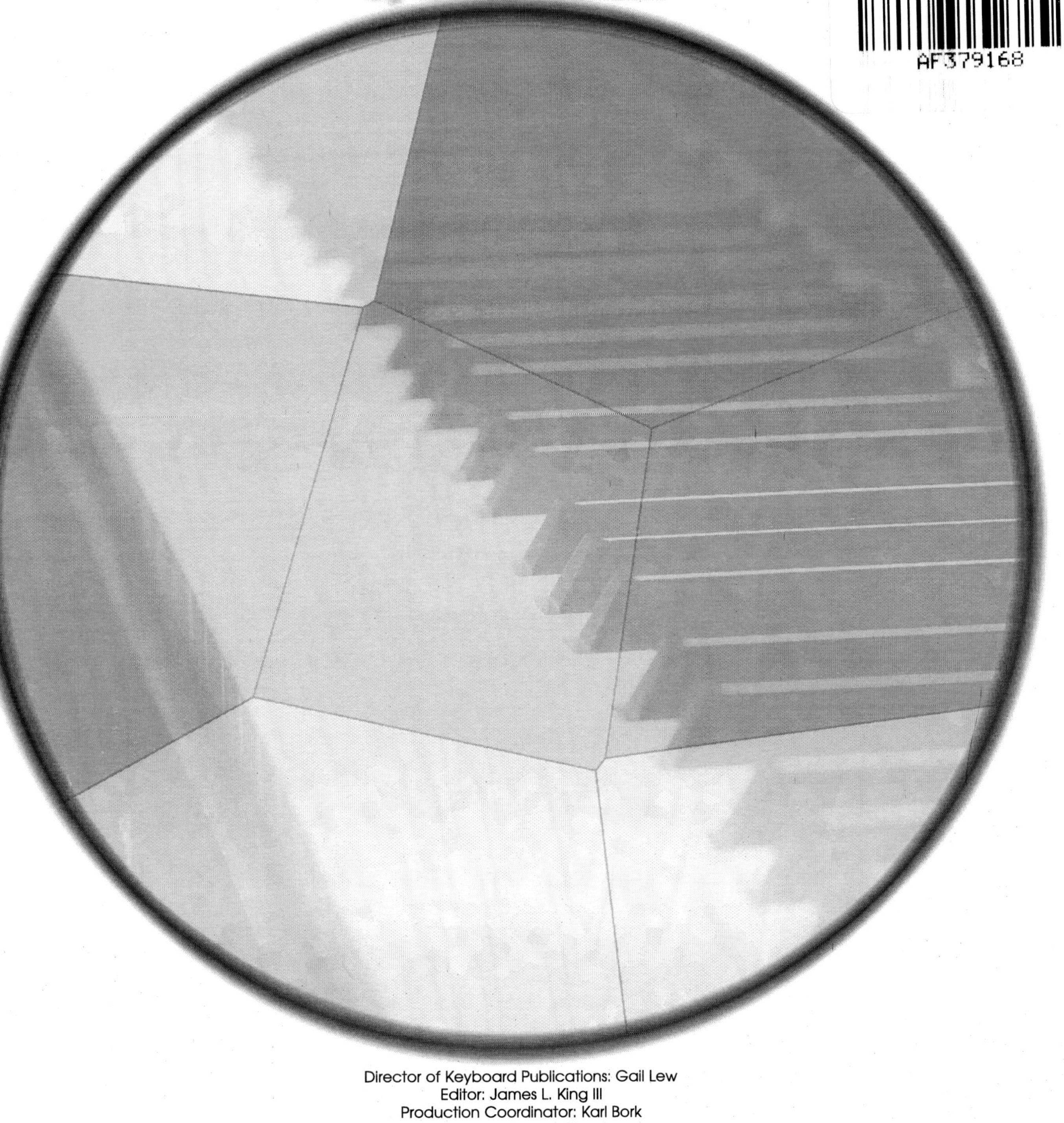

Director of Keyboard Publications: Gail Lew
Editor: James L. King III
Production Coordinator: Karl Bork
Art Design: Ernesto Ebanks

Contents

Preface

Jazz artists learn their art by listening, playing, and improvising on standard tunes. Improvisation is a creative process that depends on many personal factors such as inventiveness and technical ability. This jazz series offers a good balance of standard songs and jazz originals that expose players to jazz styling at various levels of technical development and ease them into improvisation using written-out riffs and improvisations while providing chord symbols that allow players to improvise using their own ideas.

The blues is one of the fundamental roots from which all jazz has developed. Blue notes, consisting of flatted 3rd, 5th, and 7th degrees of a scale, are used extensively in "Bluesy" on page 5, "Upbeat Monday" on page 8, and "Nocturne" on page 28. One important feature in "Jazzy Waltz" is its syncopated rhythm (see measures 8, 12, 20, and 23). The remaining pieces are jazz standards using traditional jazz harmonies. Written-out improvisations that contain many blue notes are included. The chord symbols will help identify the altered tones and can also be used as an aid to improvisation. To create your own blues sound, try playing the first three notes of a minor scale or an interval of a minor 3rd when experimenting with your own harmonizations.

(continued on page 4)

Preface

(continued from page 4)

You do not have to stay strictly in the key, however. For example, the notes C and E♭ are part of a C blues scale. If you play these notes over a D7 chord, you will hear a bluesy sound even though C and E♭ are not the blue notes for the key of D.

Developing your own melodic ideas in improvisation is achieved in different ways. In jazz, performers take a song and put their own stamp on it by composing their own ideas based on a chord sequence or a tonality, manipulating the original harmonies, or changing the style of the composer's original treatment of the song. The rhythmic element in jazz improvisation cannot be stressed enough: A musical motive might be accented in a different way, rhythmically altered (as in swing eighths), played at a higher or lower pitch, transposed to a different chord, or repeated as a sequence with a similar contour but using different notes. The possibilities are completely open to the creativity of the performer.

Larry Minsky

Bluesy

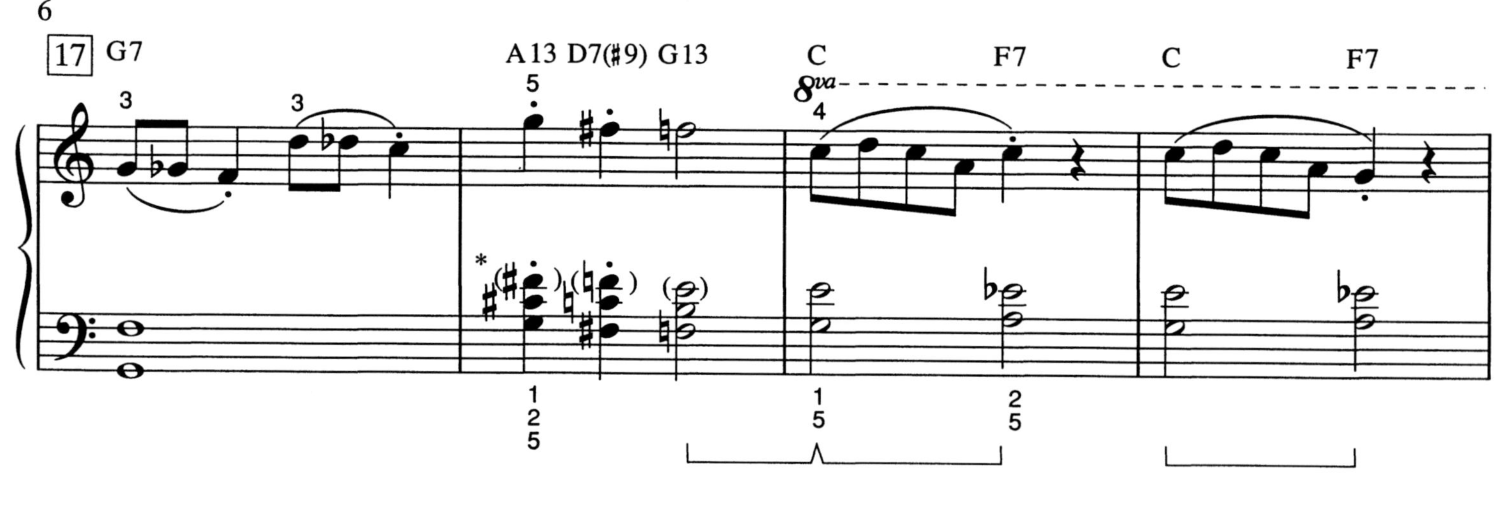

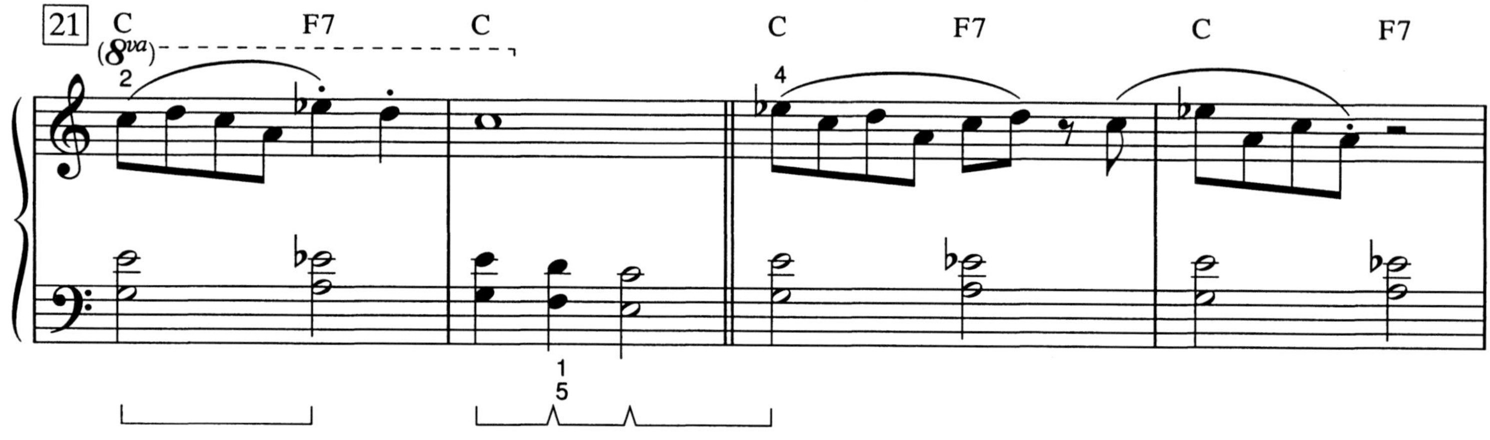

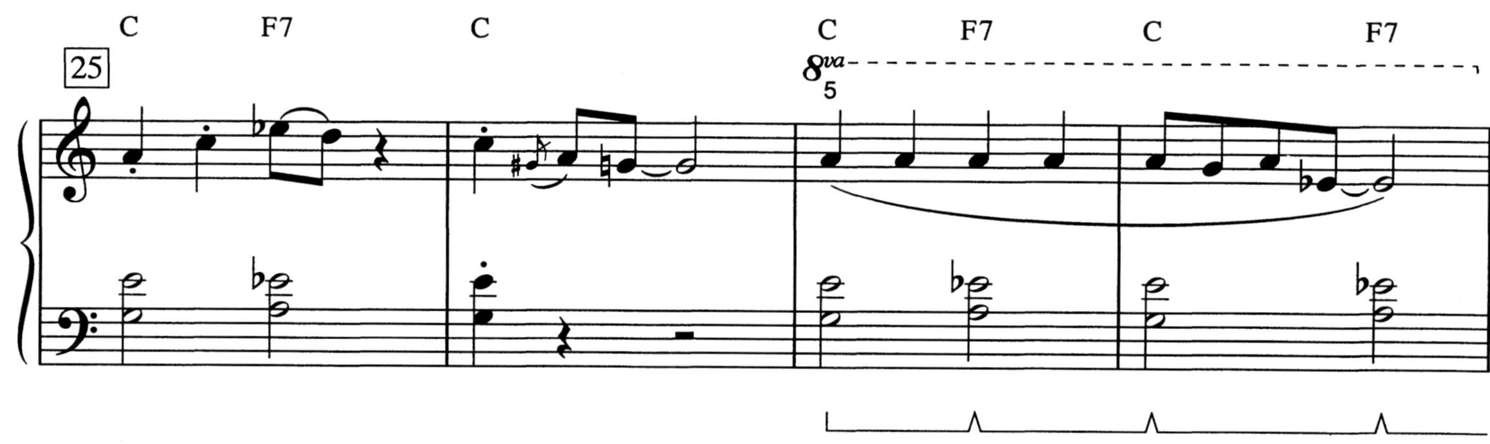

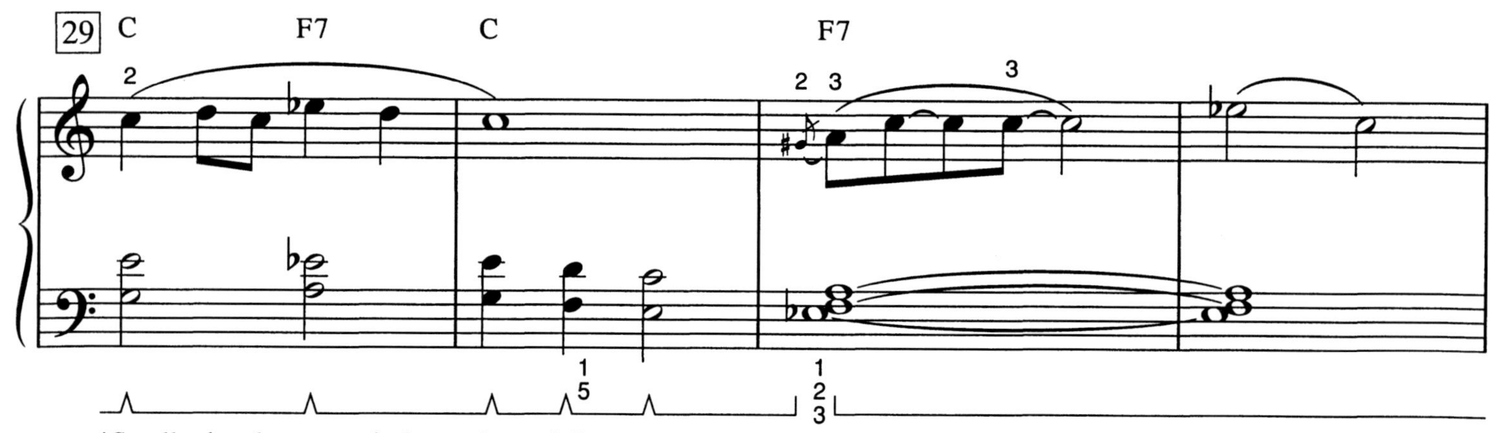

*Smaller hands may omit the top bass clef notes.

ELM02023

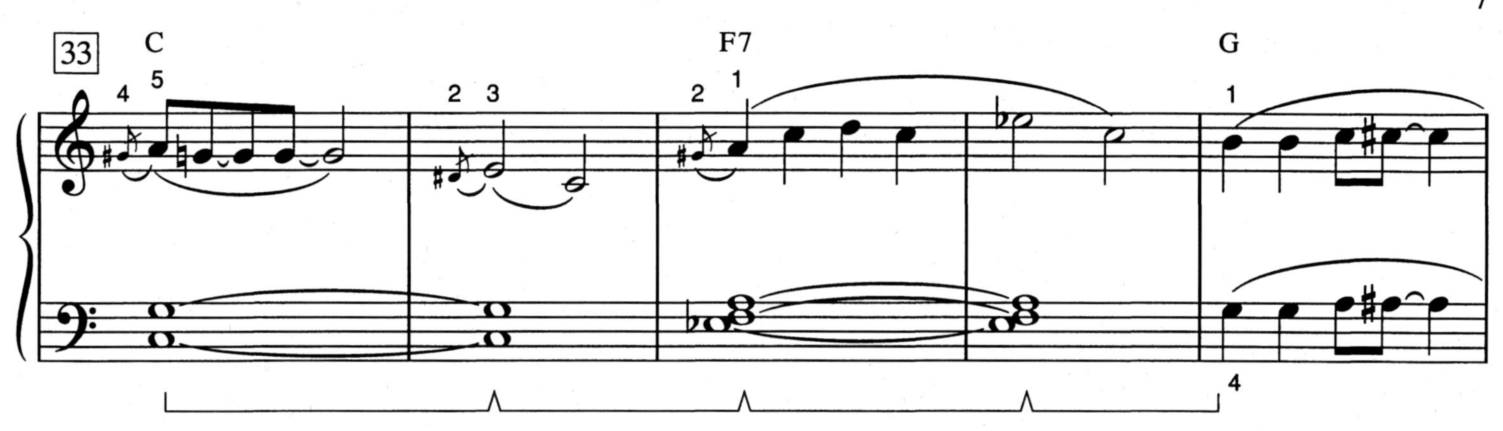

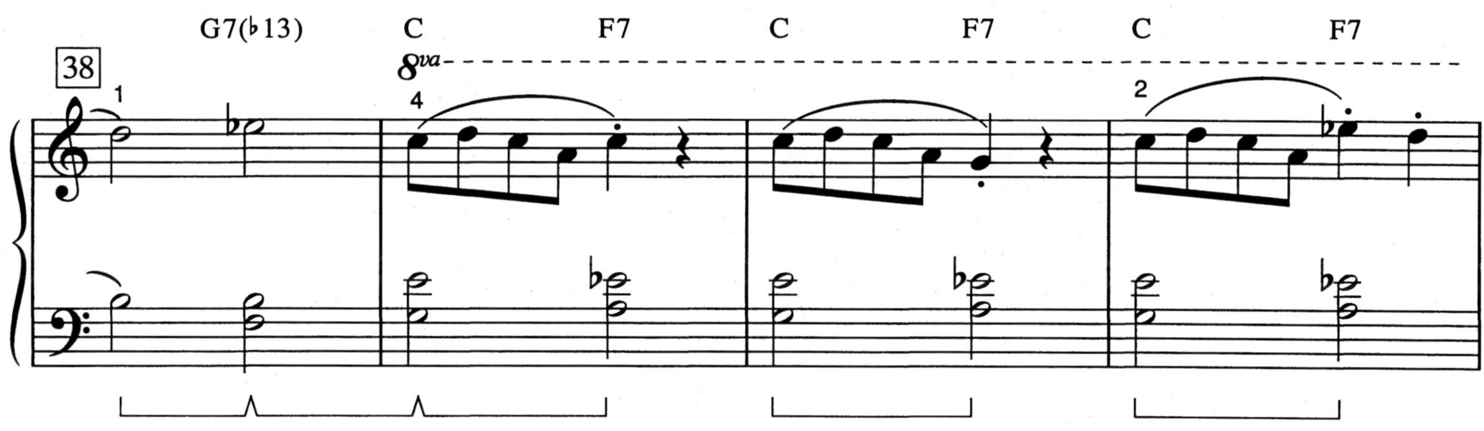

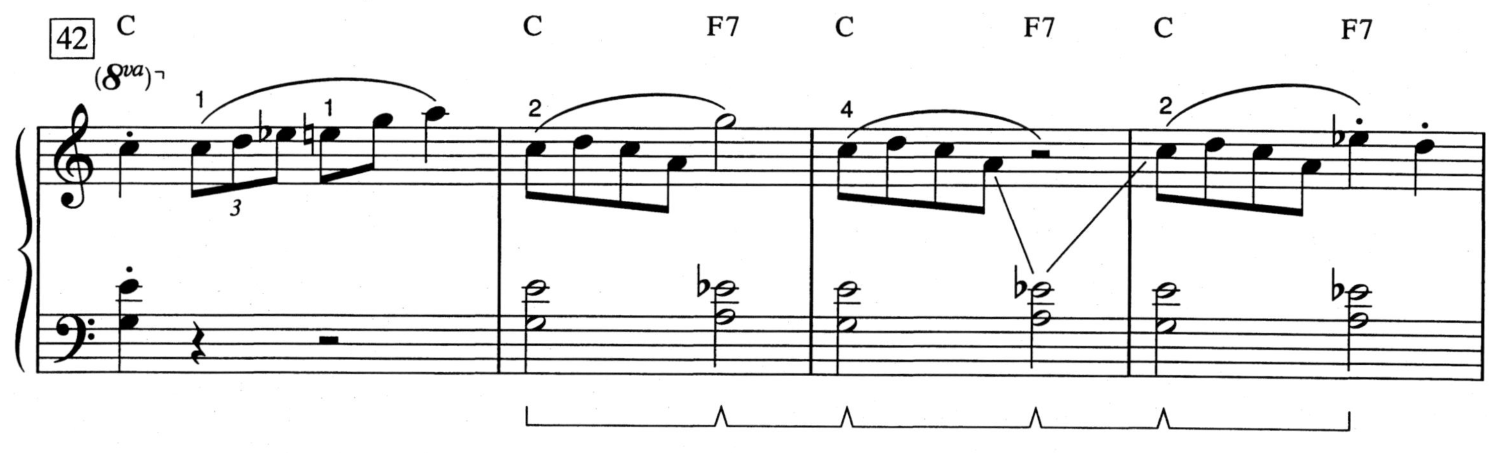

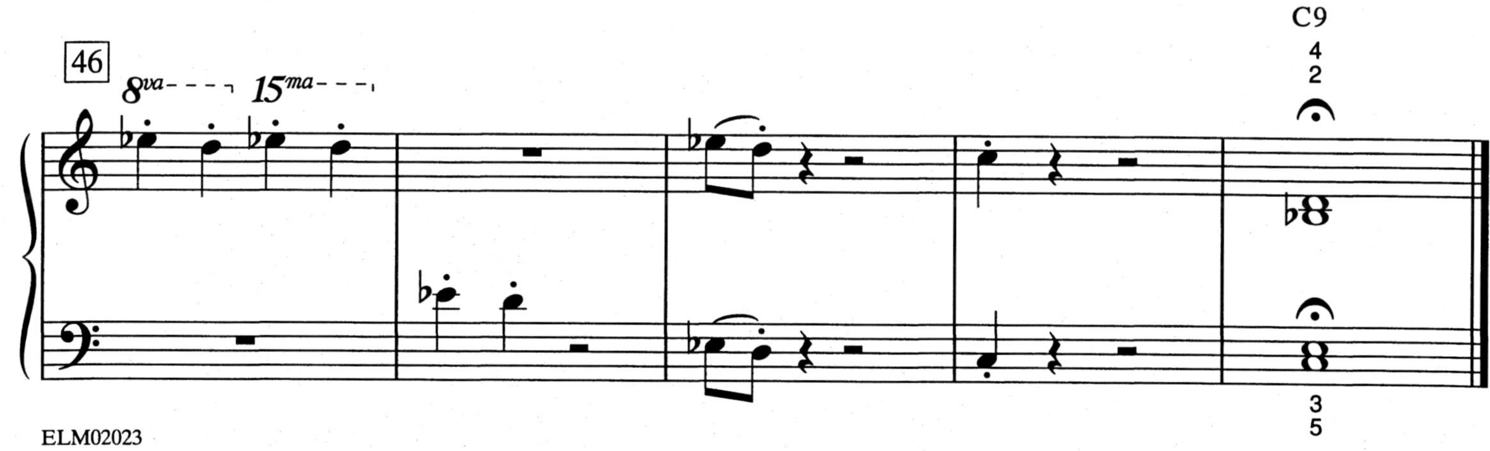

Upbeat Monday

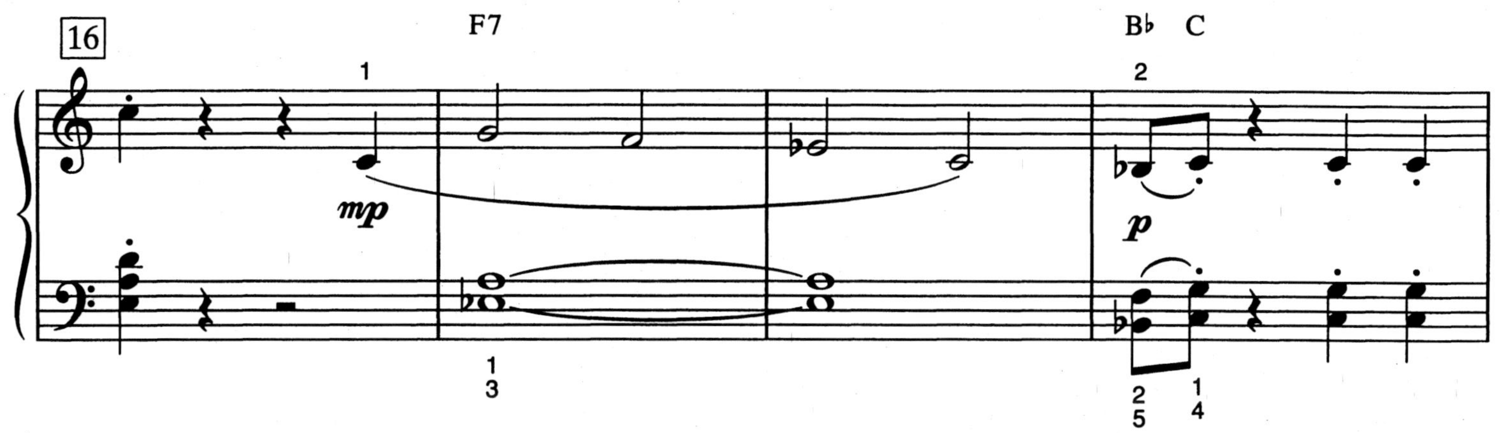
16
F7
B♭ C
mp
p

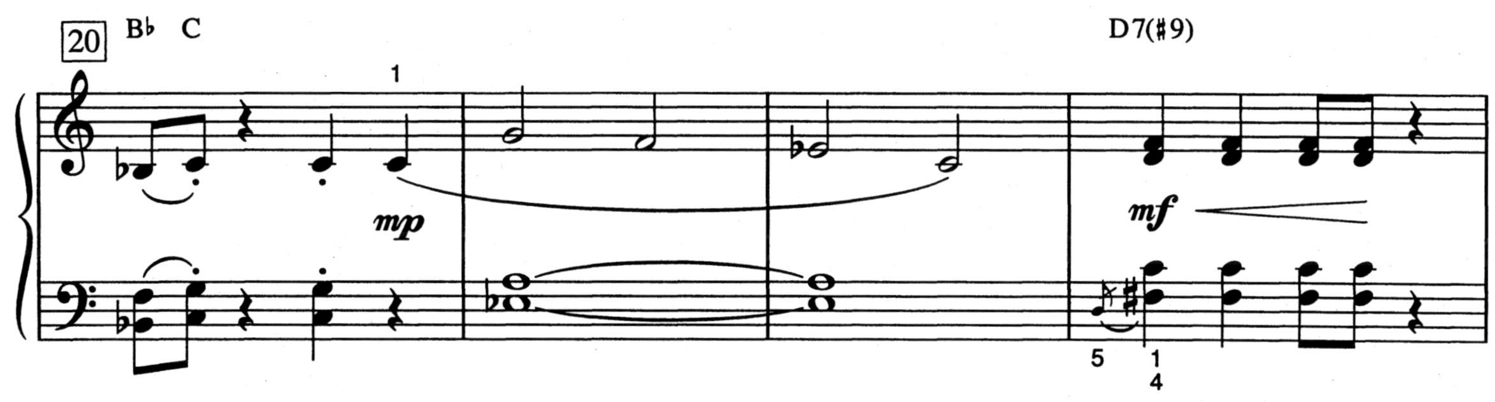
20
B♭ C
D7(♯9)
mp
mf

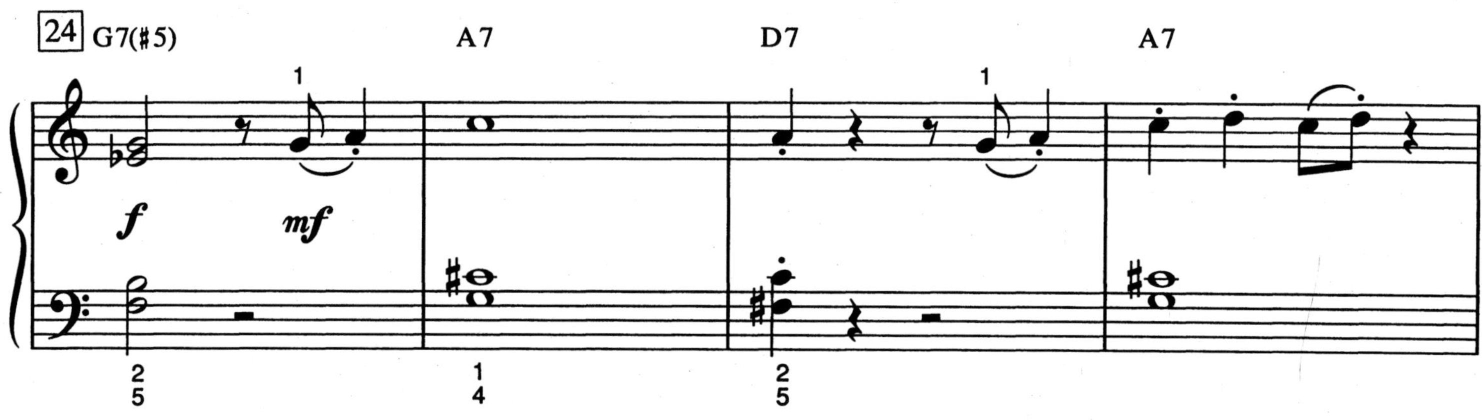
24
G7(♯5)
A7
D7
A7
f
mf

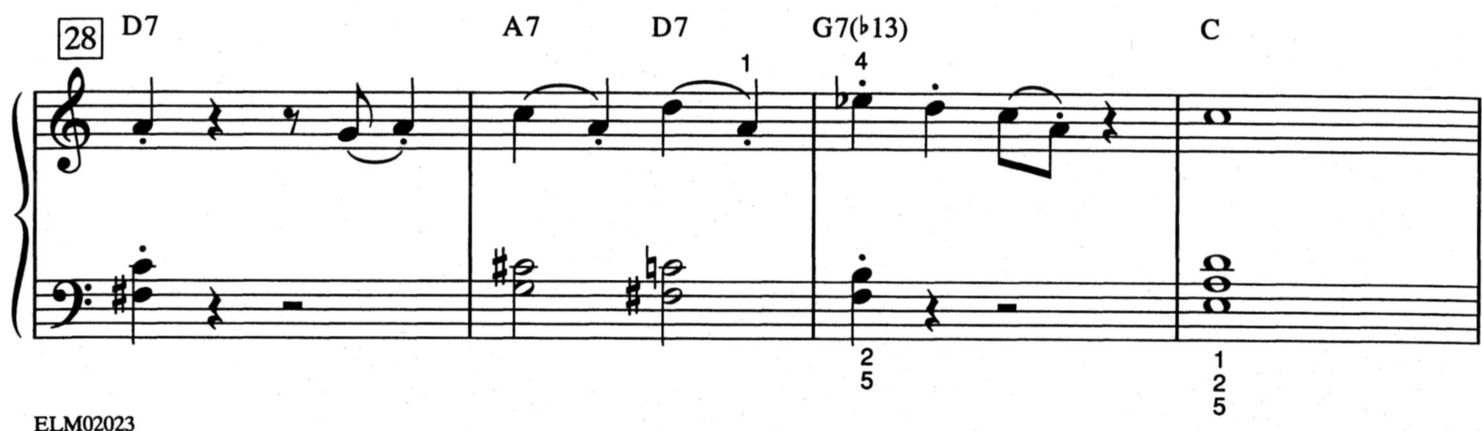
28
D7
A7
D7
G7(♭13)
C

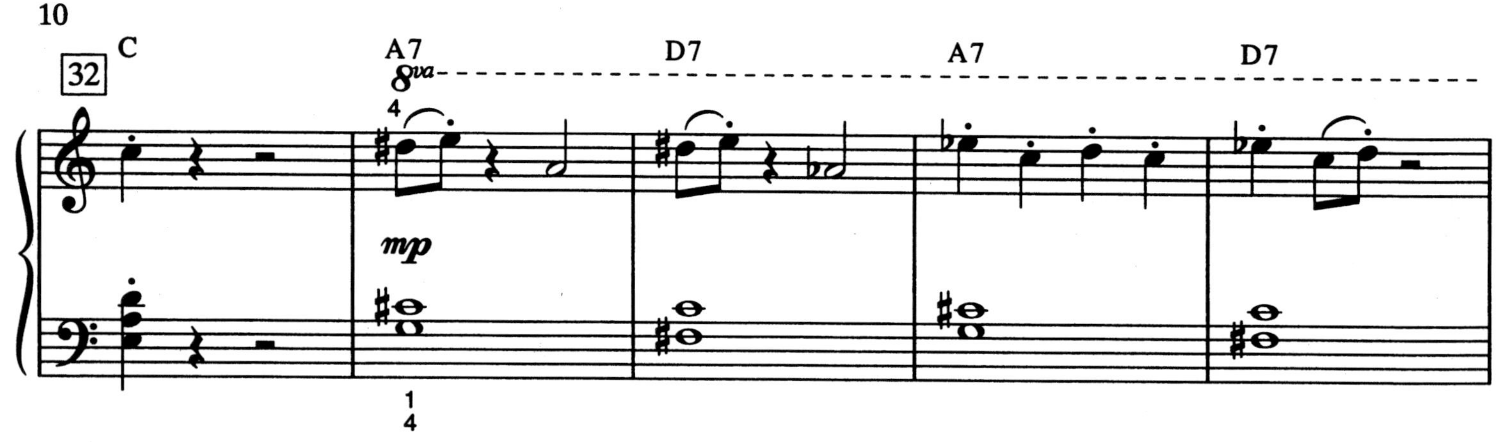

10
32
C
A7
D7
A7
D7
8va
4
mp
1
4

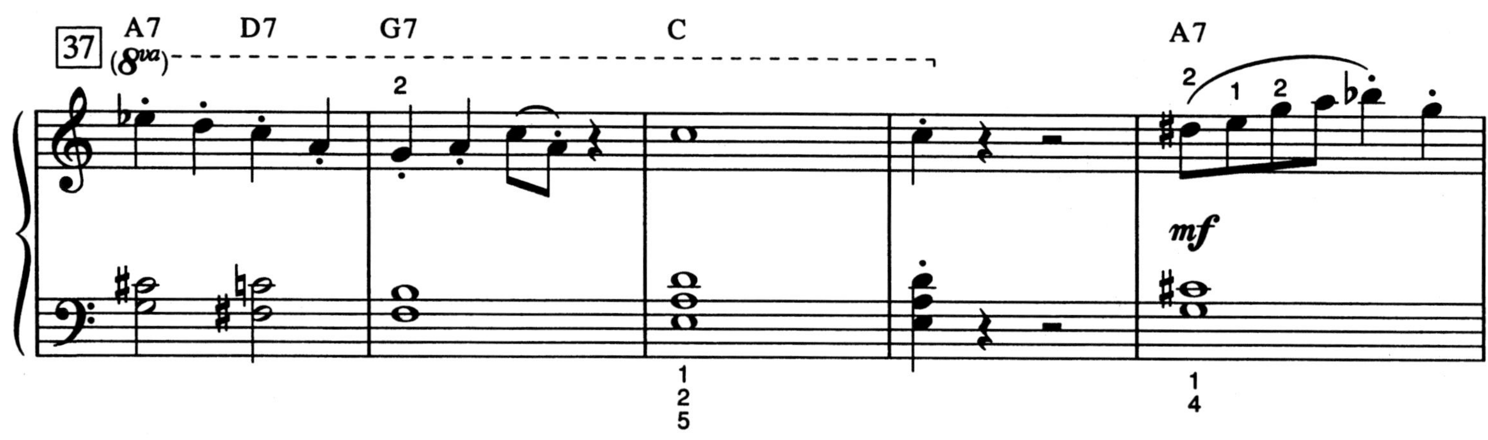

37
A7
D7
G7
C
A7
(8va)
2
2
1
2
mf
1
2
5
1
4

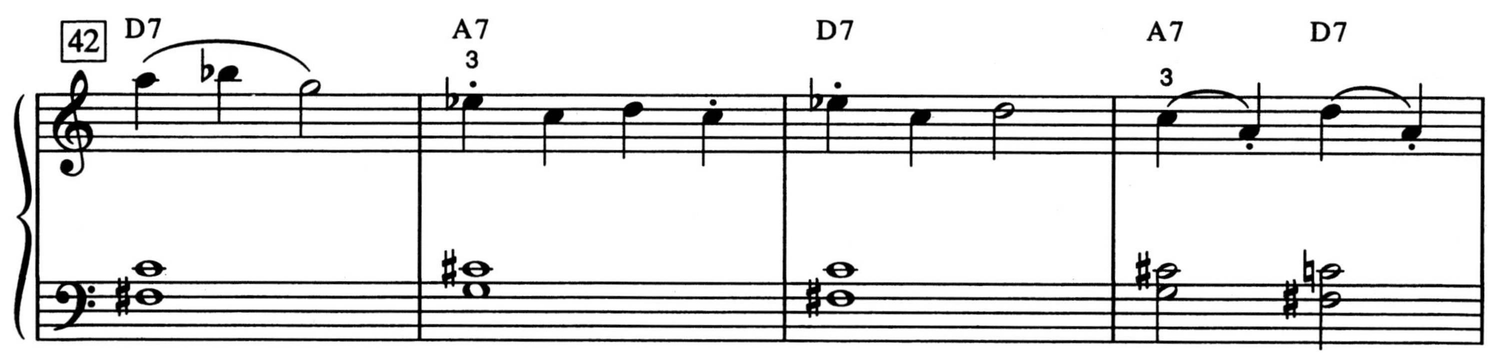

42
D7
A7
D7
A7
D7
3
3

46
G7
C
F7
4
2
3
p
1
2
5
1
3

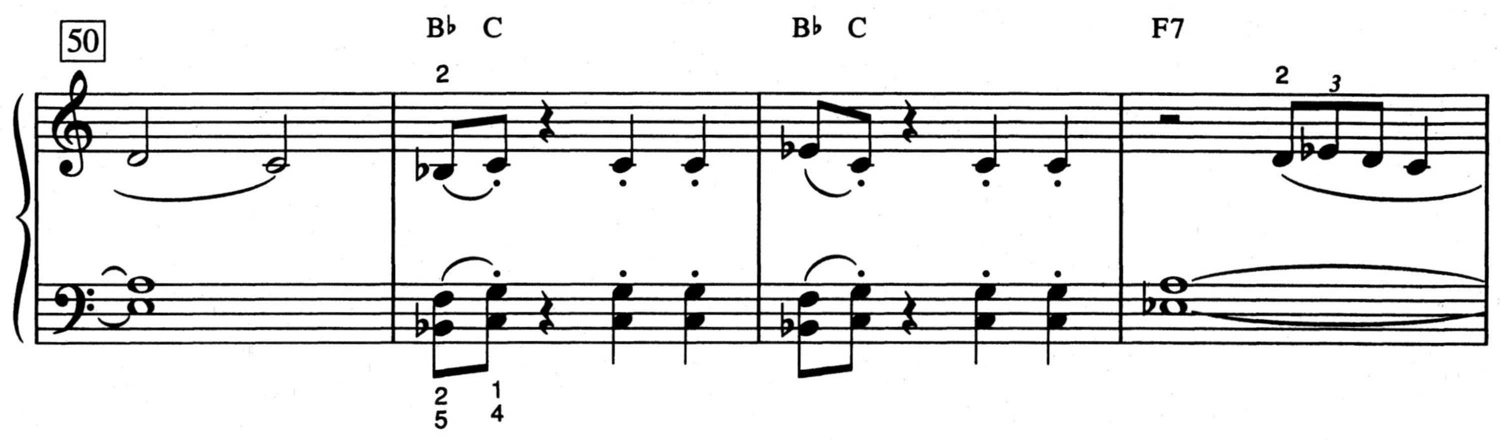
50
B♭ C
B♭ C
F7

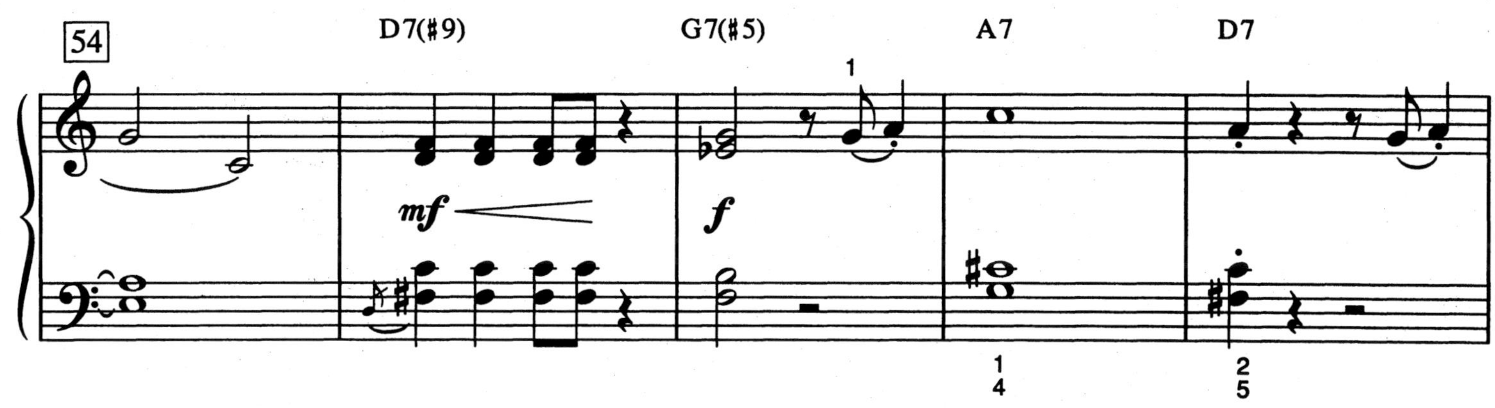
54
D7(♯9)
G7(♯5)
A7
D7
mf
f

59
A7
D7
A7
D7
A7
D7
8va

63
G7
8va
C
8va

Jazzy Waltz

LARRY MINSKY

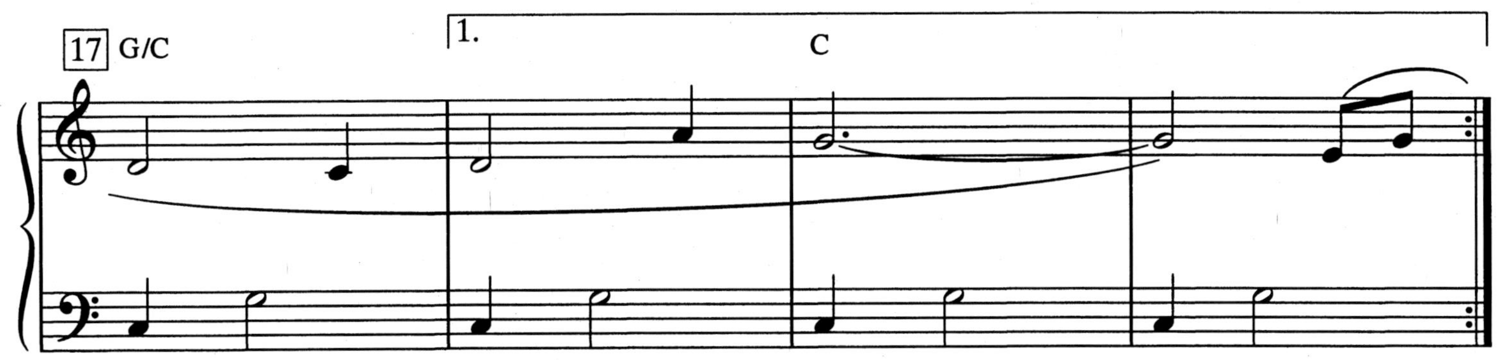
17 G/C
1.
C

2.
21 G
C
B♭add9

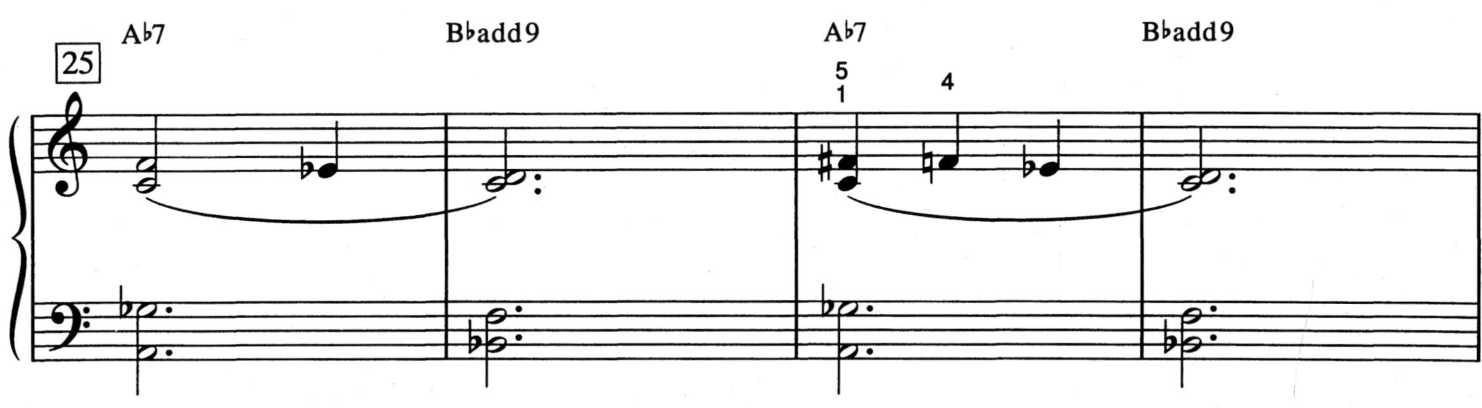
A♭7
B♭add9
A♭7
B♭add9
25
5
1
4

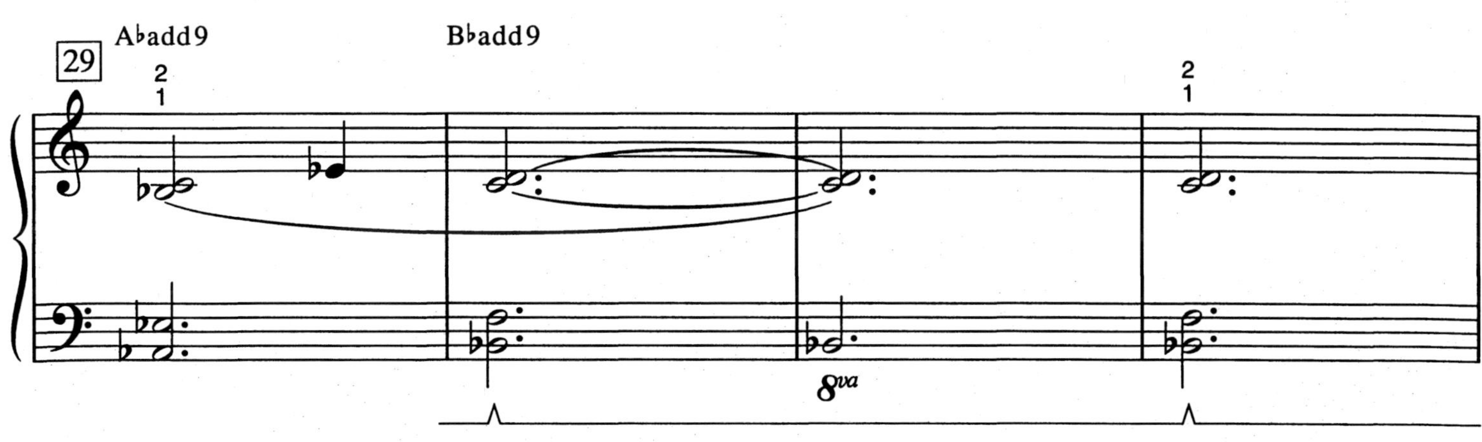
A♭add9
B♭add9
29
2
1
2
1
8va

33
A♭7
B♭add9
A♭7
B♭add9
5
1
pedal simile

37
A♭add9
B♭add9
B♭
A♭add9
8va
5
3
5
3
2

42
B♭
A♭add9
B♭
A♭
B♭add9
8va

47
C5
(C5)
D.S. al Coda
pedal simile

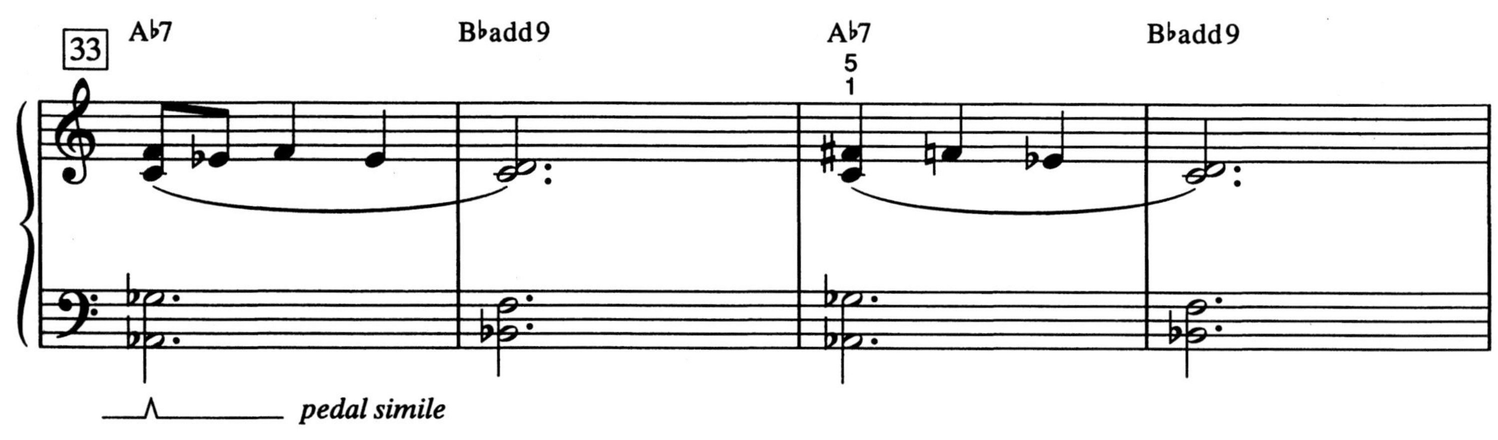

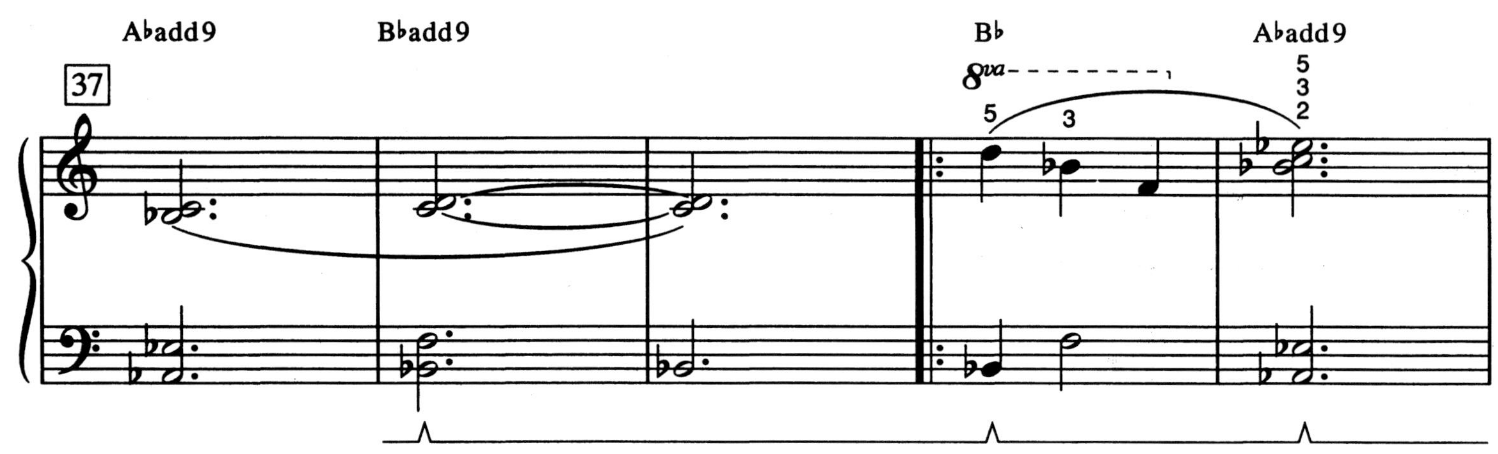

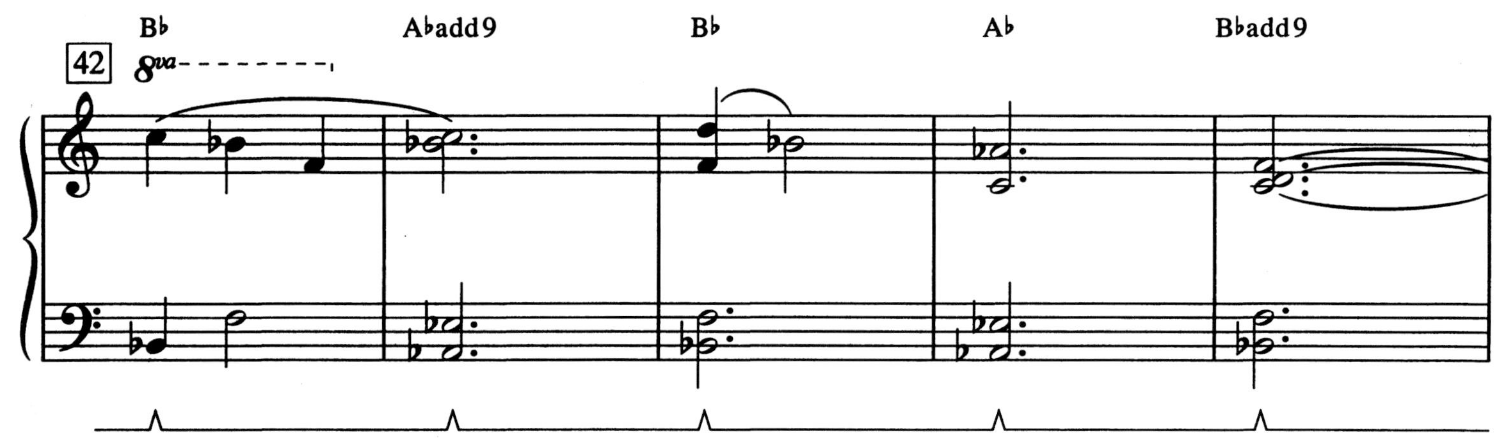

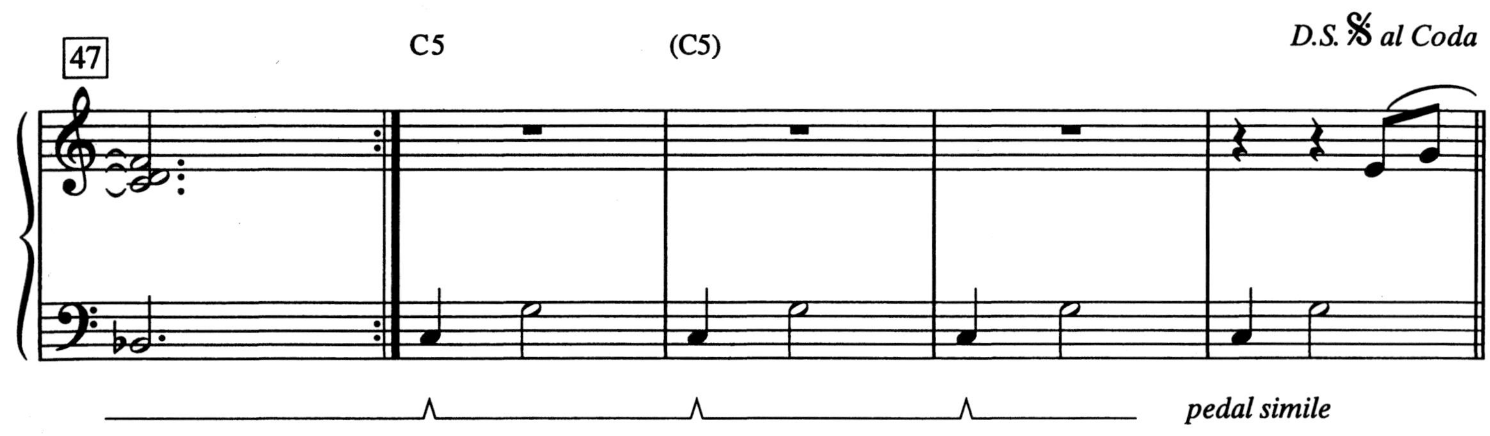

ELM02023

Coda
52
Cmaj7
F13
Cmaj9
D7(#9)
G/C

57
C
G/C
1
rit. e decresc.

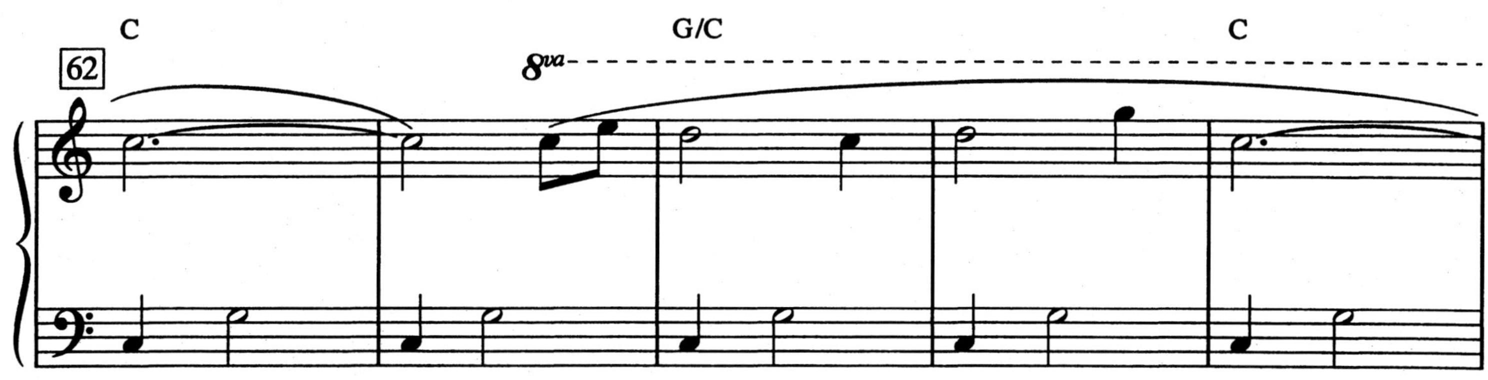
C
62
8va
G/C
C

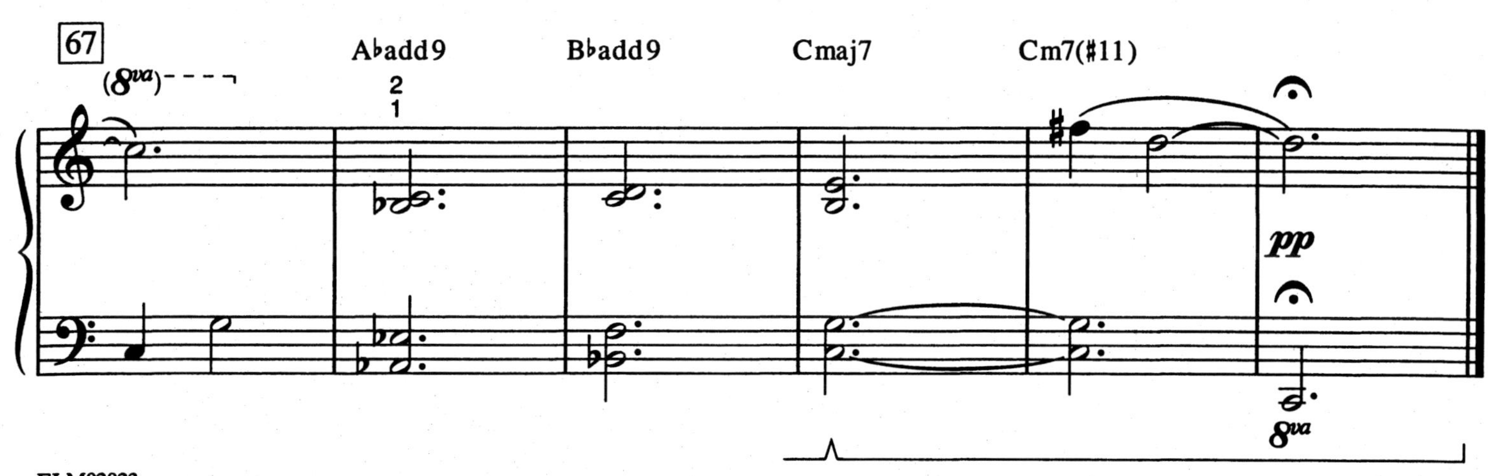
67
(8va)
Abadd9
2
1
Bbadd9
Cmaj7
Cm7(#11)
pp
8va

How Long Has This Been Going On?

Music and Lyrics by
GEORGE GERSHWIN and IRA GERSHWIN
Arranged by LARRY MINSKY

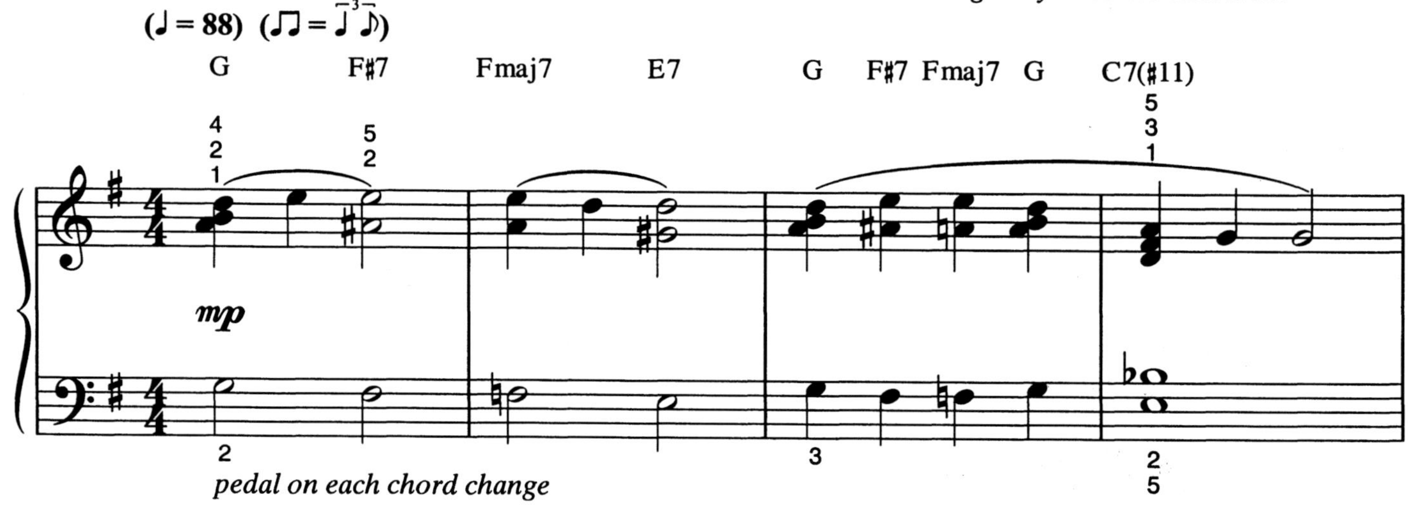

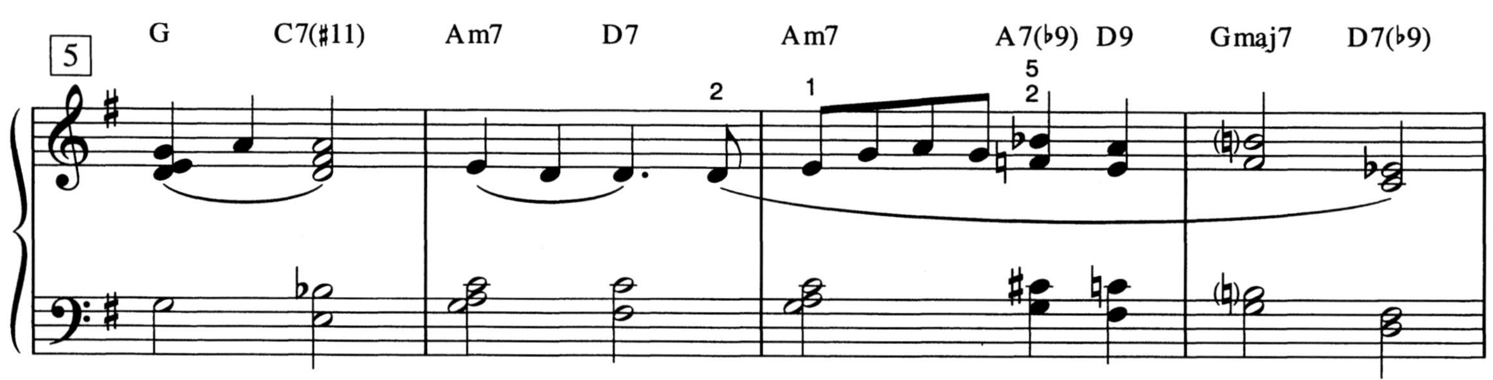

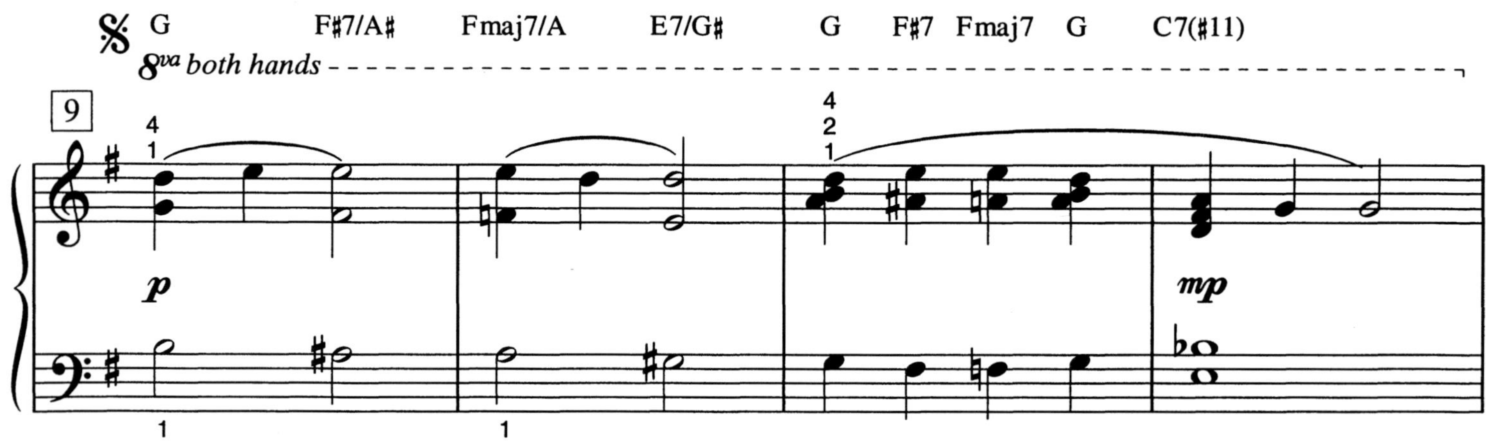

To Coda
13
G   C7(#11)   Am7   D7   Am7   A7(b9) D9   Gmaj7   B7
17
Em   F7   Em   Em   F7   Em
mf
D.S. al Coda
21
B   F#7   Bm   F#7   Bm   F#7   Am11   D7(b9 b5)
rit.
Coda
Bm   E7(#9)   Am   A7(b9) D9   Abmaj7 Gmaj7
8va
mf   rit. e decresc.   pp
8va
ELM02023

On the Sunny Side of the Street

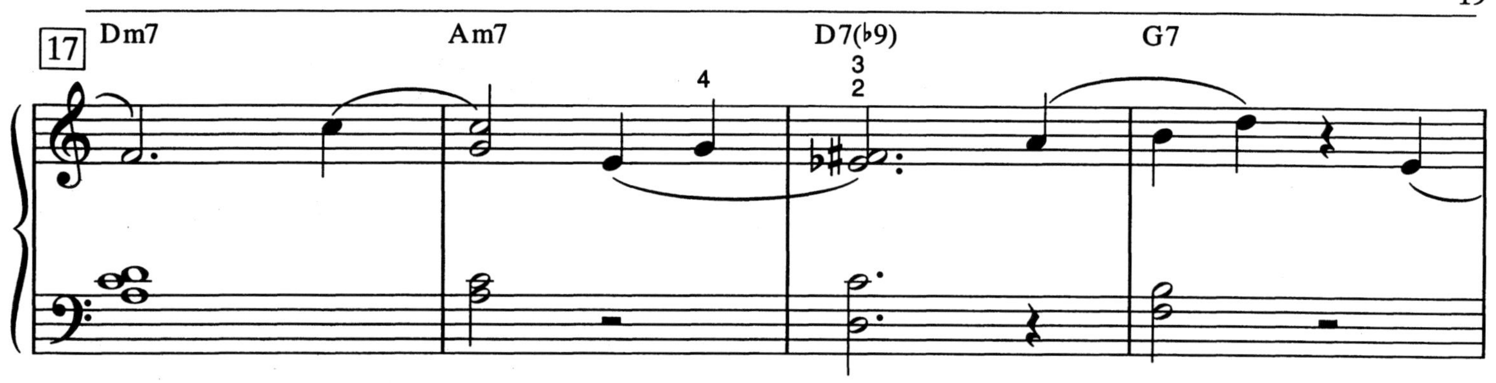
17
Dm7
Am7
D7(♭9)
G7
4
3
2

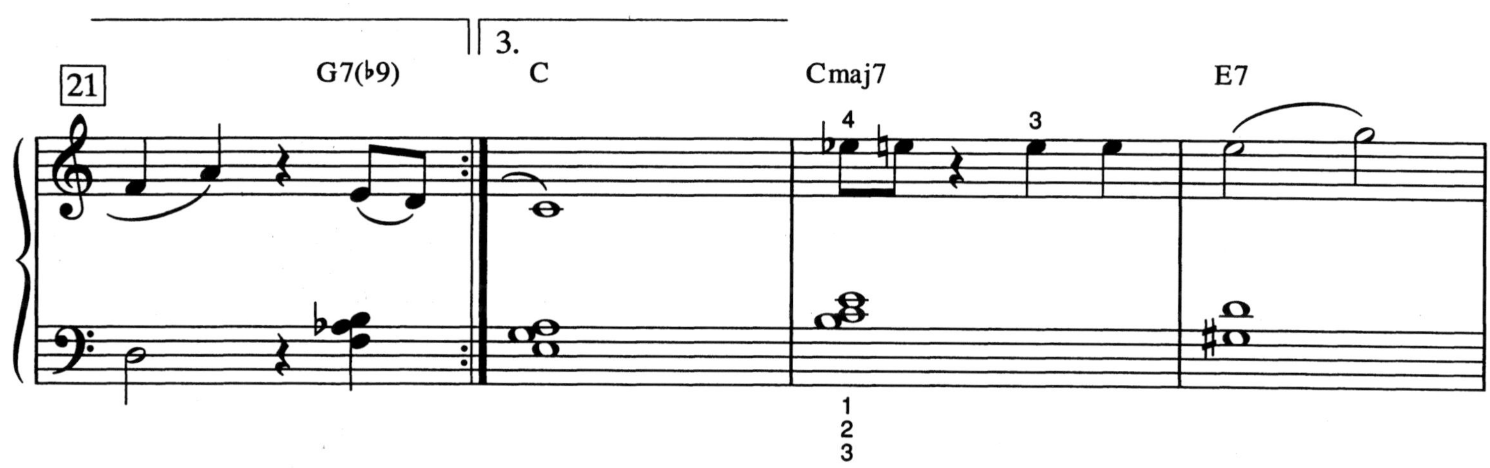
3.
21
G7(♭9)
C
Cmaj7
E7
4
3
1
2
3

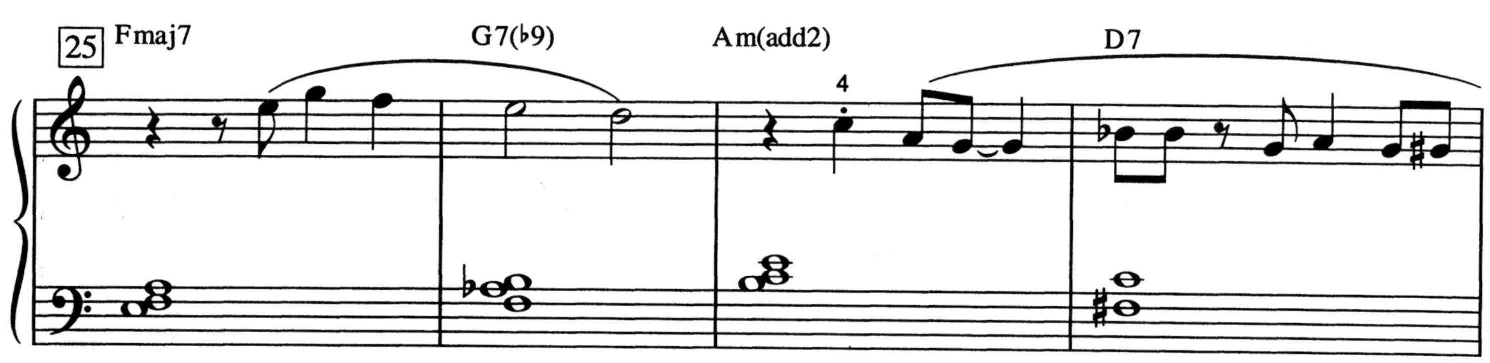
25
Fmaj7
G7(♭9)
Am(add2)
D7
4

Dm7
G7
Cmaj7
Cmaj7
E7
29
1
1
1
3

33
Fmaj7
G7(♭9)
Am
D7
1

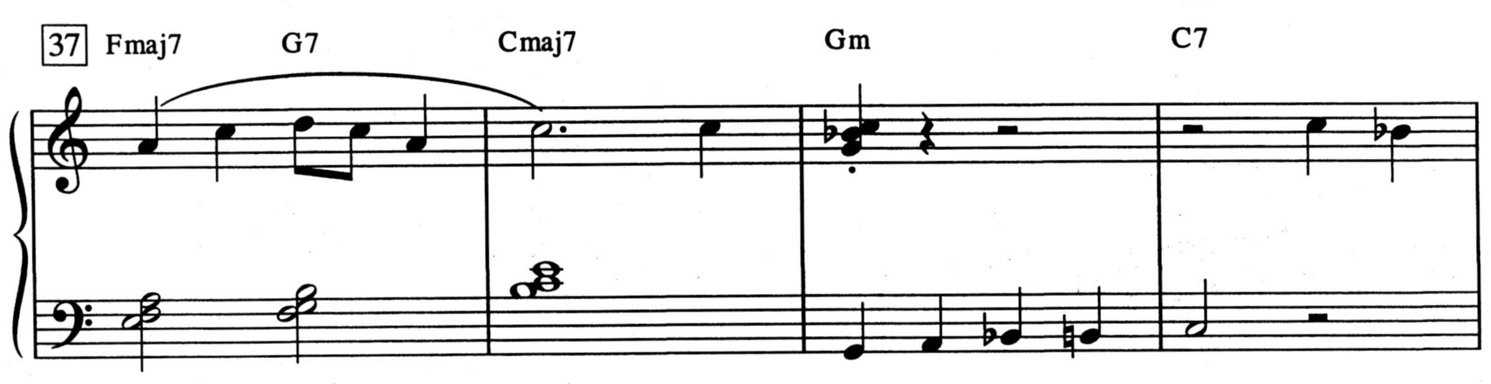
37
Fmaj7
G7
Cmaj7
Gm
C7

41
F
2
Am7
D7
5
5

G7
C
E7(♯9)(♯5)
45
1 2
1 3
1
3
1
5
3
1
2
3
5

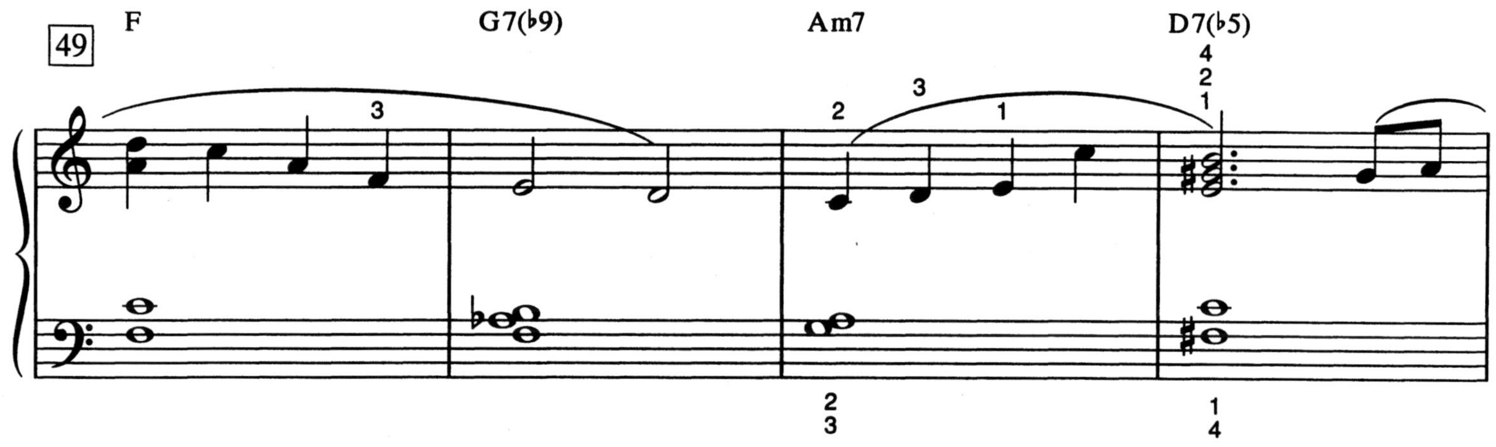
49
F
G7(♭9)
Am7
D7(♭5)

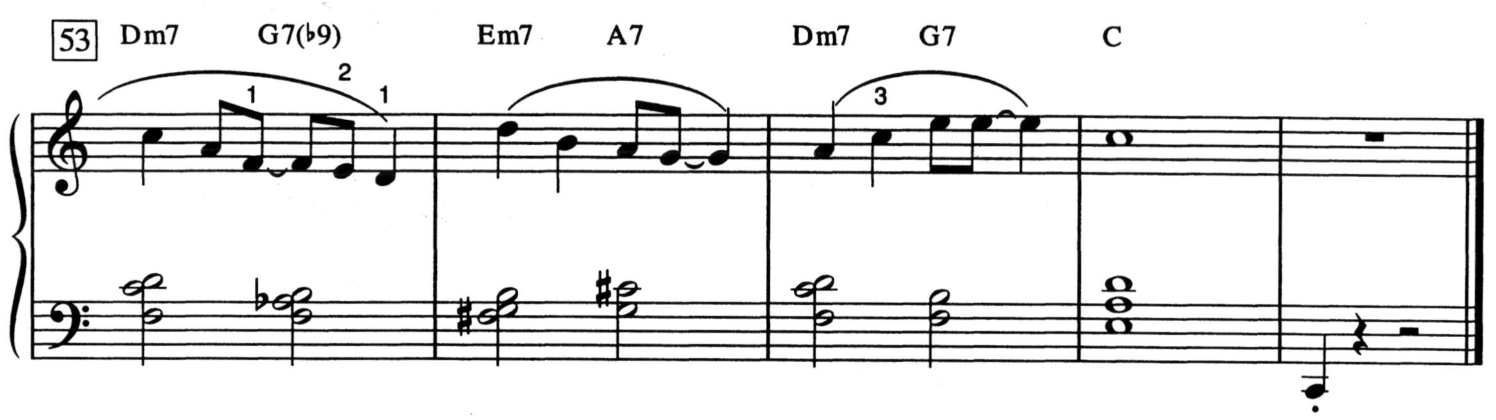
53
Dm7
G7(♭9)
Em7
A7
Dm7
G7
C

I Could Write a Book

Words by LORENZ HART
Music by RICHARD RODGERS
Arranged by LARRY MINSKY

17 Em7   E♭11   D7(♭9)   Dm11   G7

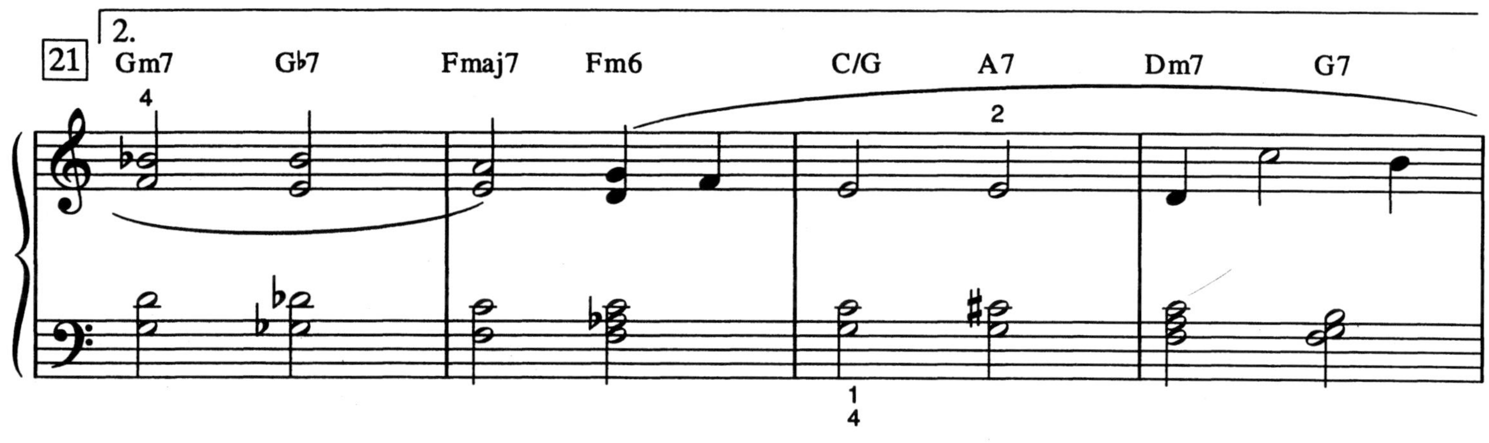
2.
21 Gm7   G♭7   Fmaj7   Fm6   C/G   A7   Dm7   G7

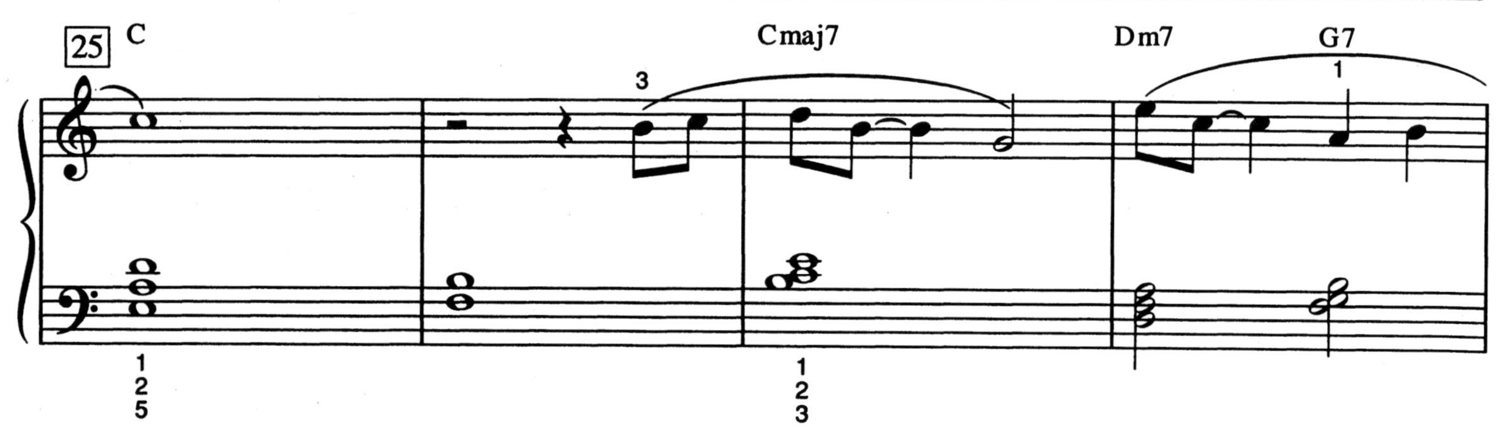
25 C   Cmaj7   Dm7   G7

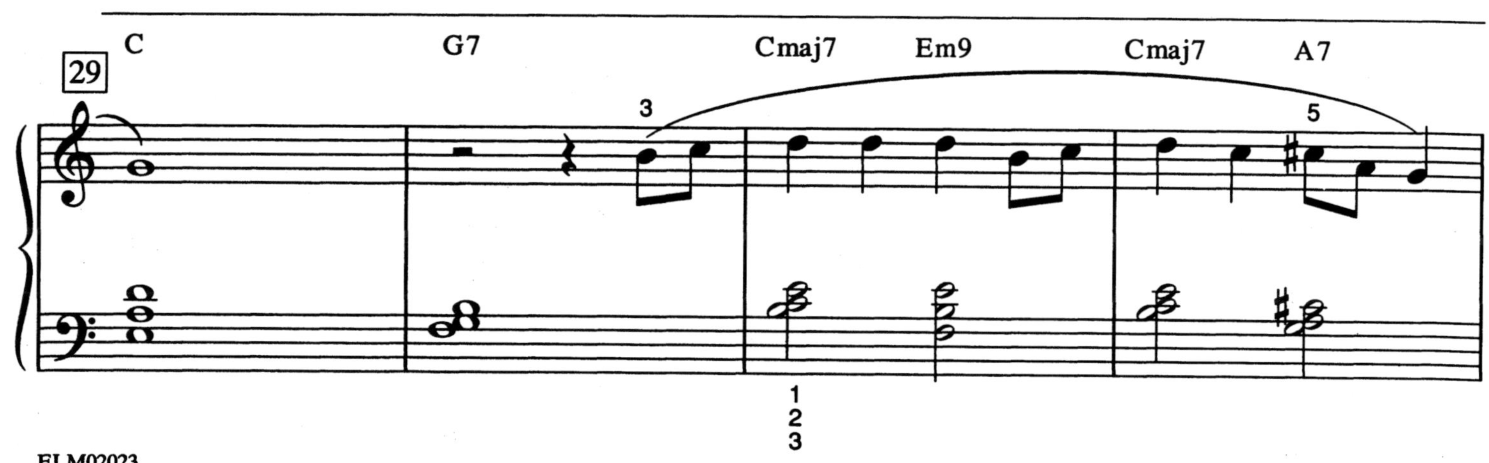
29 C   G7   Cmaj7   Em9   Cmaj7   A7

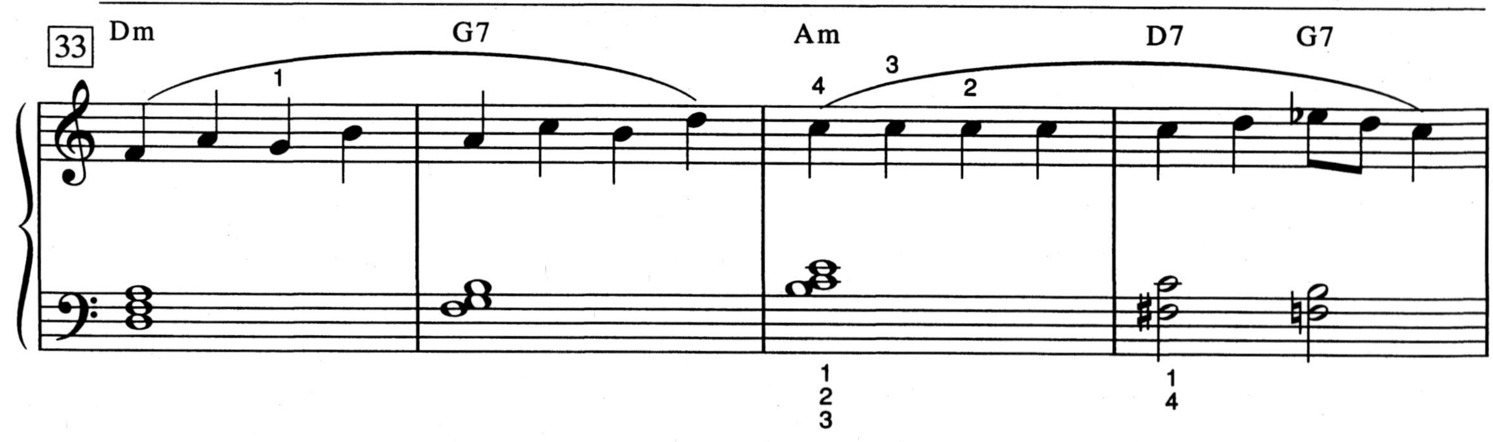
33
Dm   G7   Am   D7   G7
1
4 3 2
1
2
3
1
4

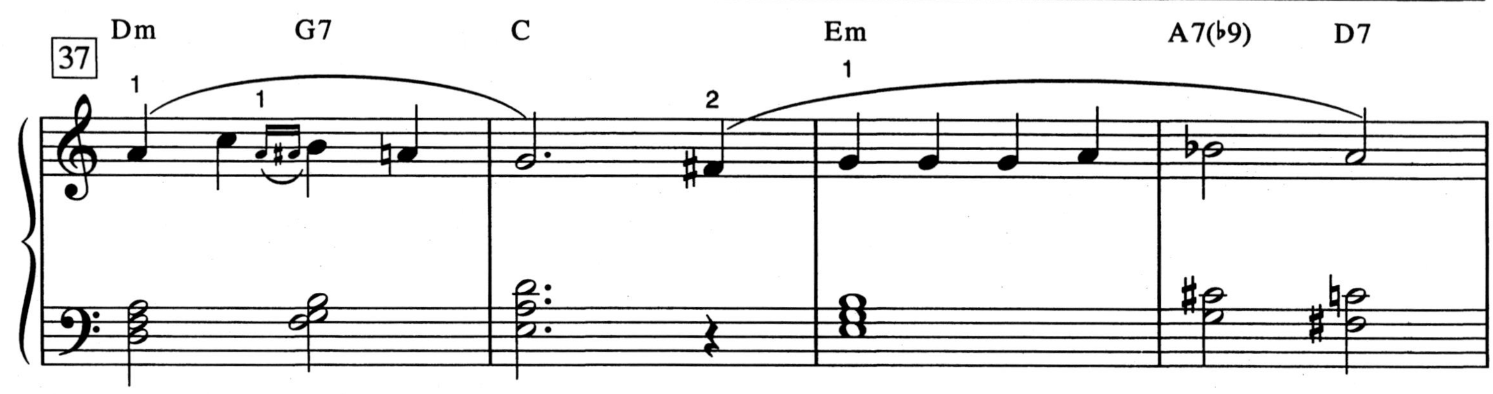
37
Dm   G7   C   Em   A7(♭9)   D7
1 1 2 1

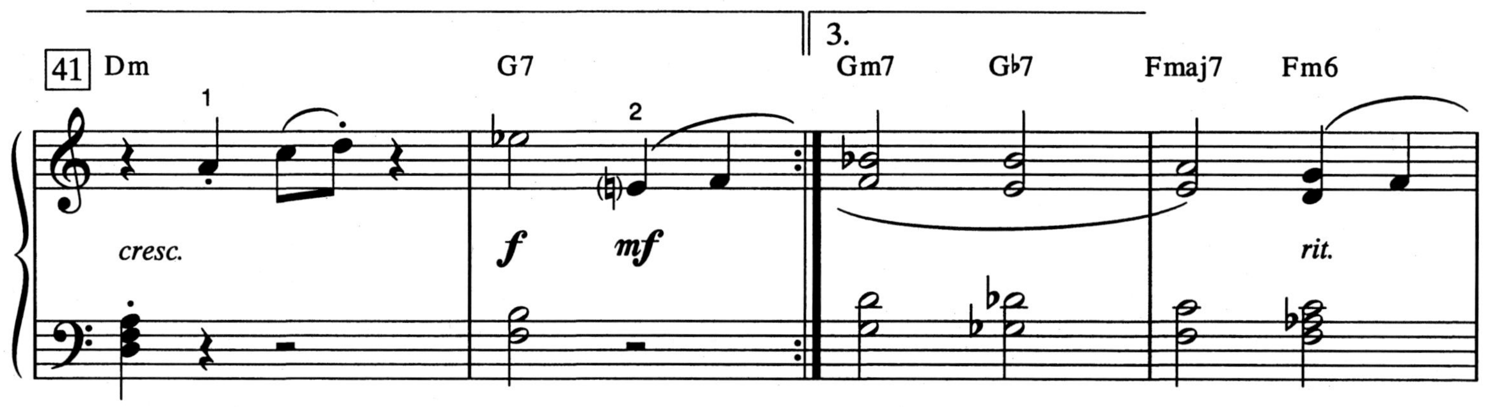
3.
41
Dm   G7   Gm7   G♭7   Fmaj7   Fm6
1 2
cresc.
f   mf
rit.

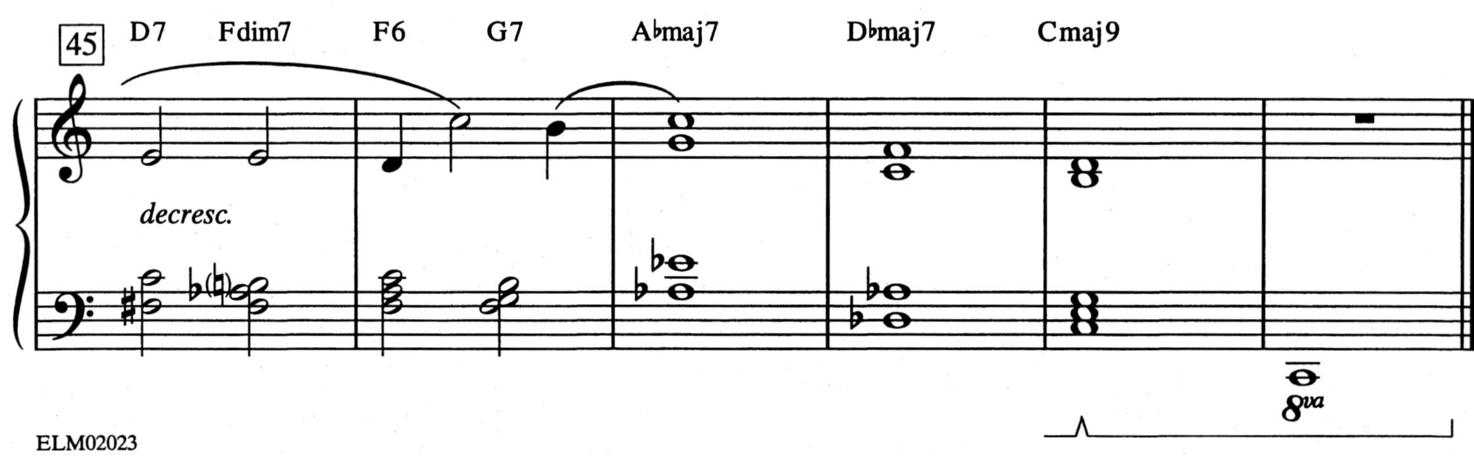
45
D7   Fdim7   F6   G7   A♭maj7   D♭maj7   Cmaj9
decresc.
8va

Over the Rainbow

Lyric by E. Y. HARBURG
Music by HAROLD ARLEN
Arranged by LARRY MINSKY

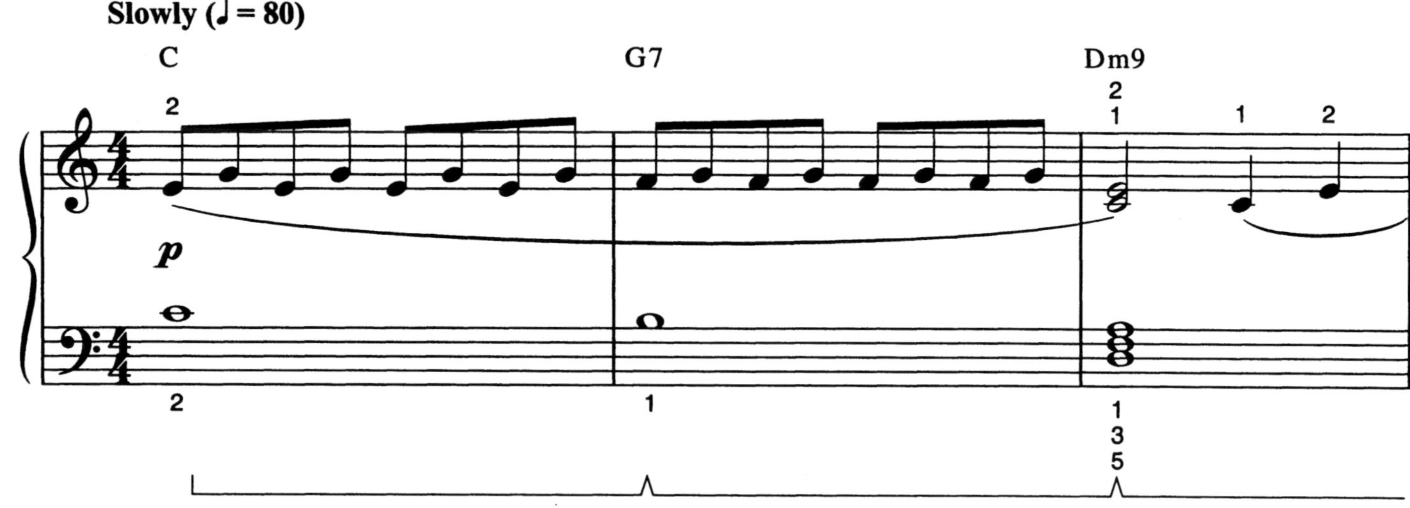

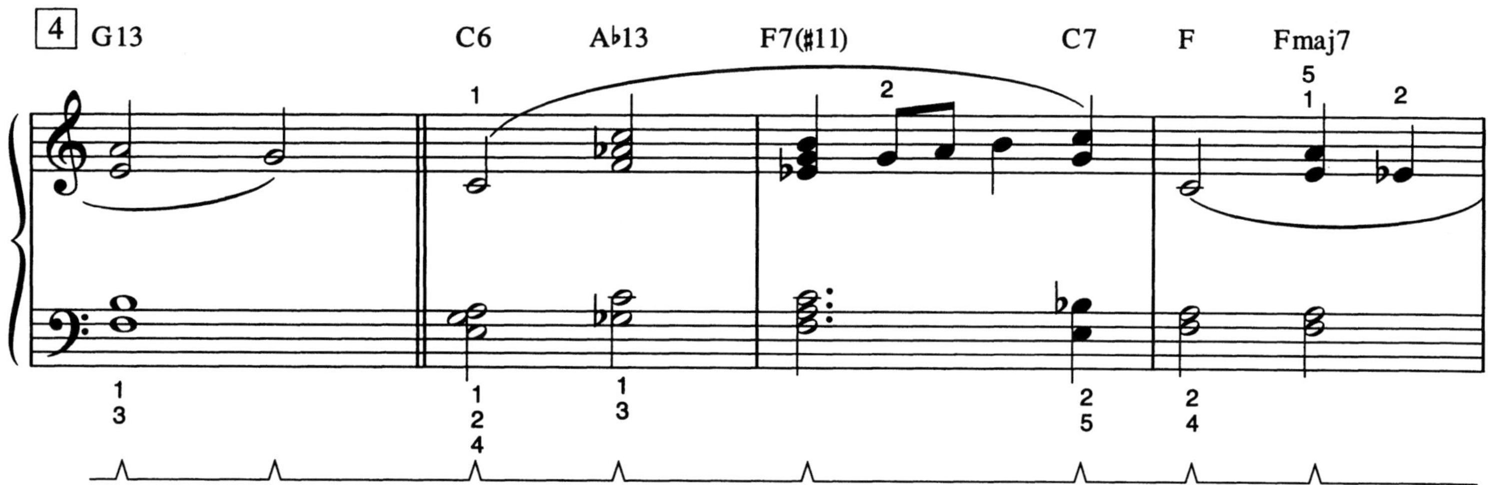

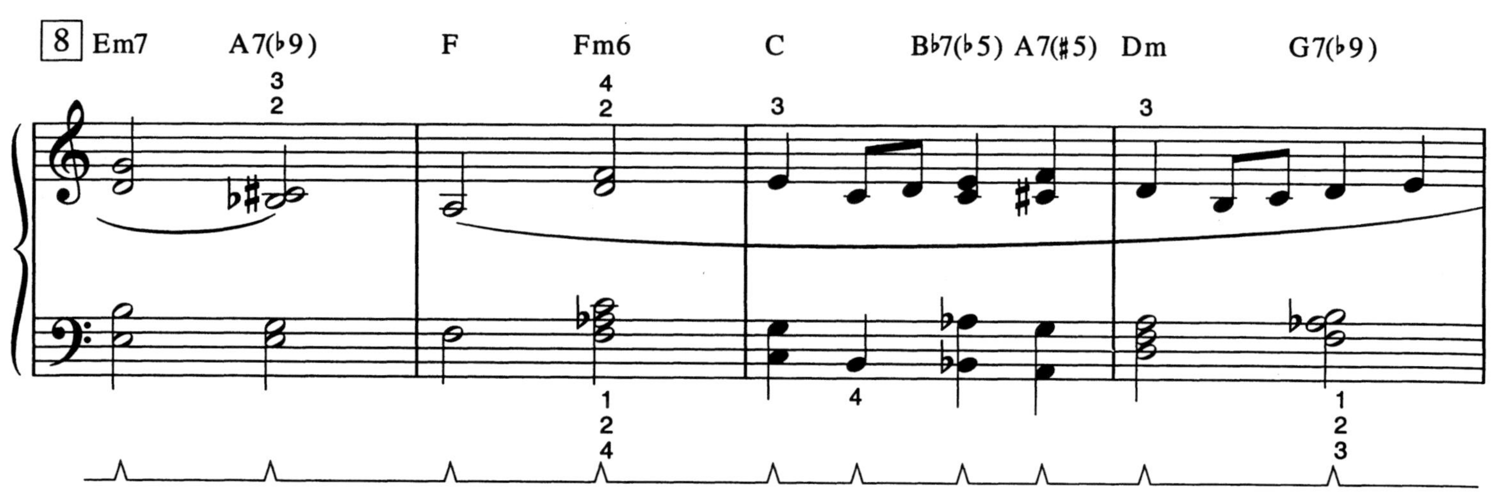

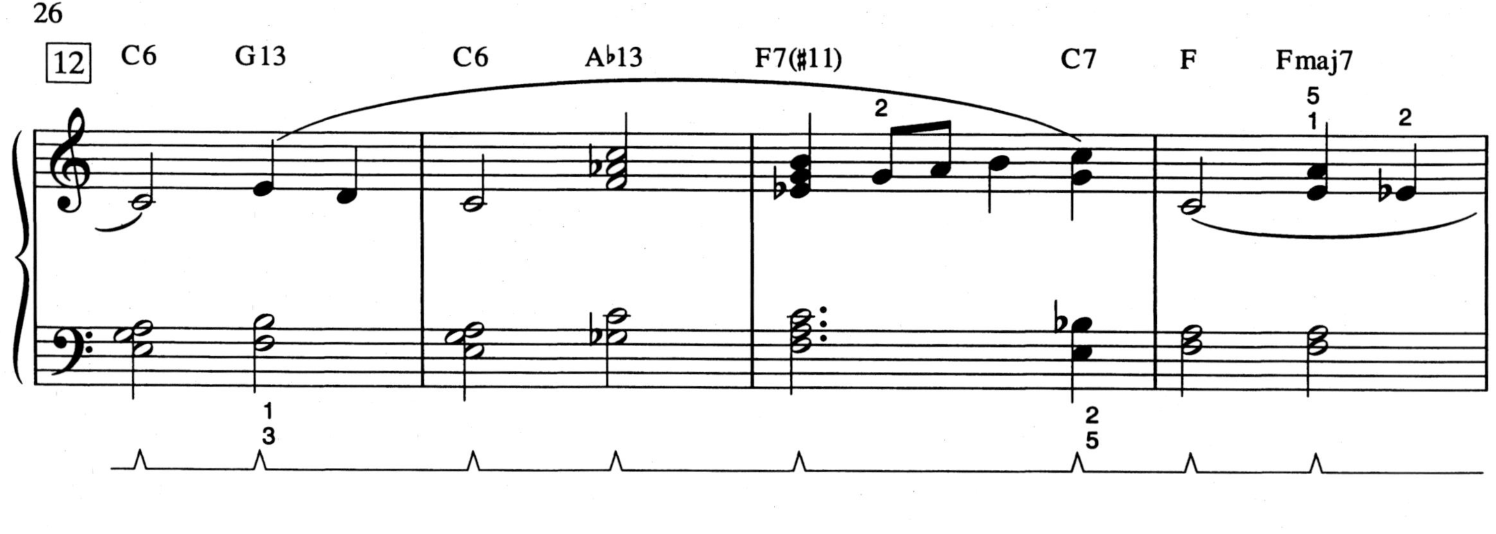
12
C6   G13   C6   A♭13   F7(♯11)   C7   F   Fmaj7

16
Em7   A7(♭9)   F   Fm6   C   B♭7(♭5) A7(♯5)   Dm   G7(♭9)

20
C6   C   Csus4   G7

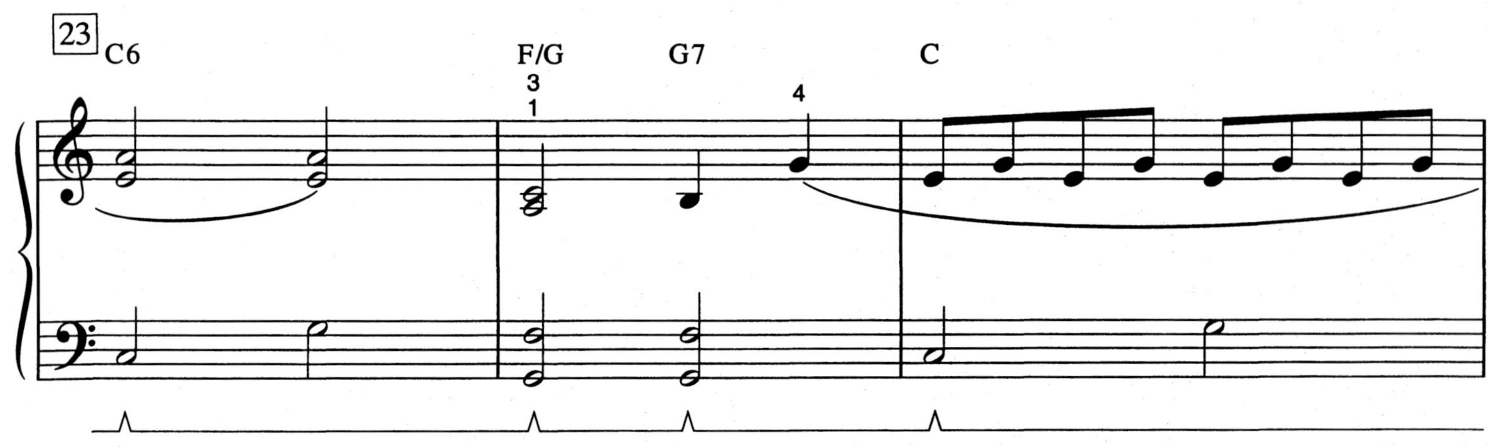
23
C6   F/G   G7   C

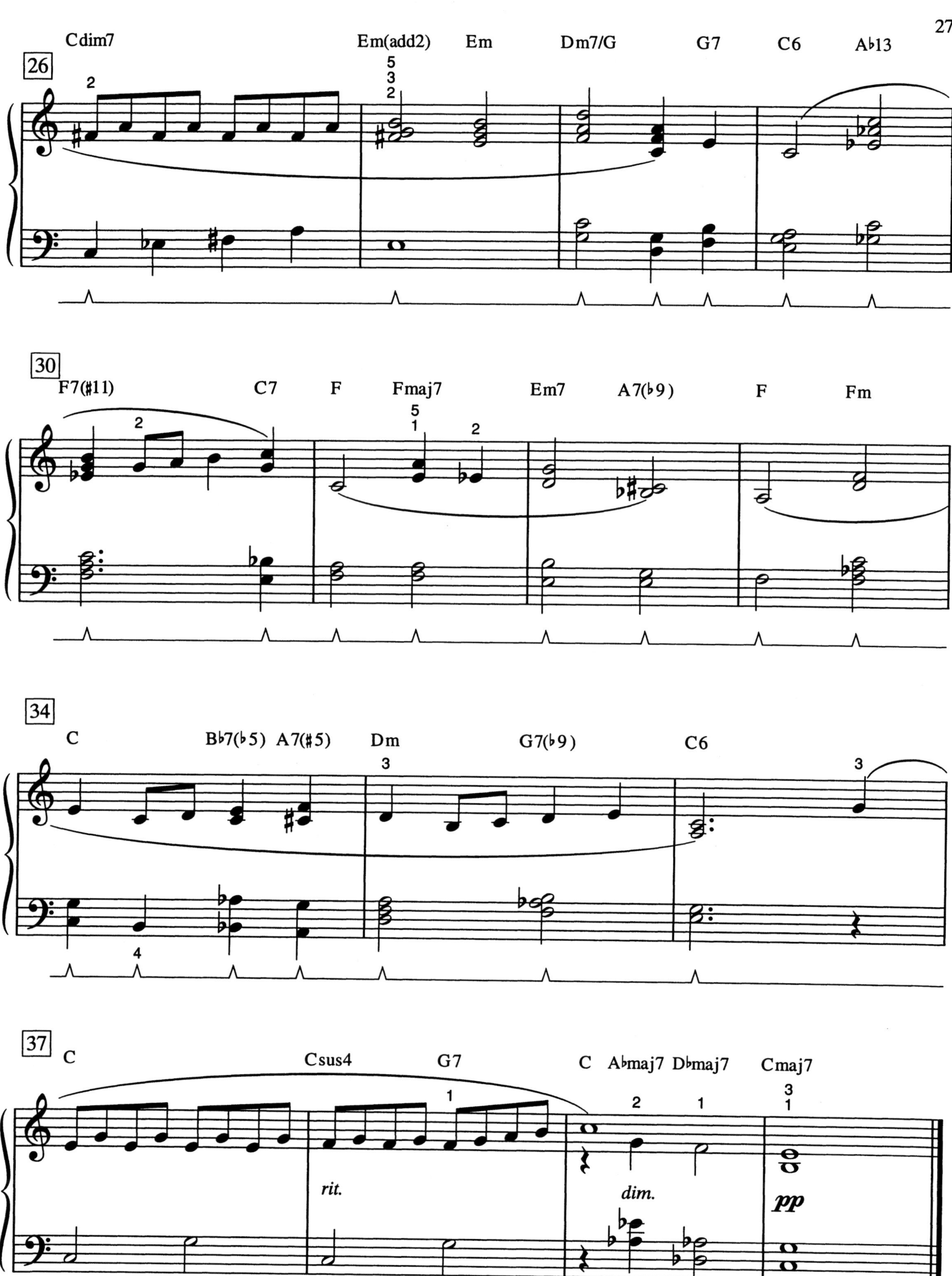

27
ELM02023

Nocturne

LARRY MINSKY

ELM02023

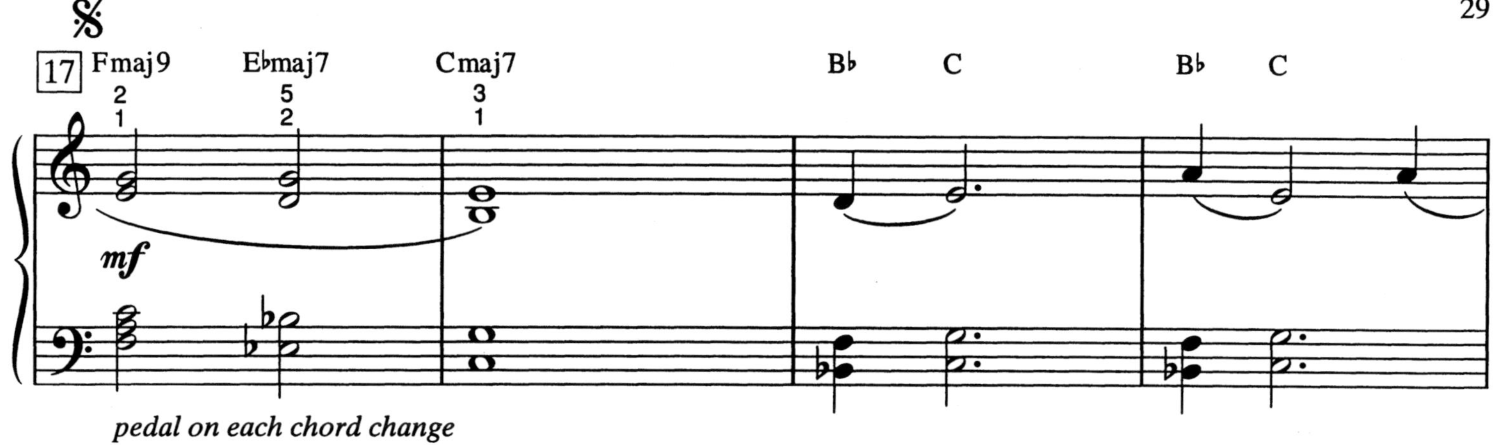
%
17 Fmaj9   Ebmaj7   Cmaj7   Bb   C   Bb   C
mf
pedal on each chord change

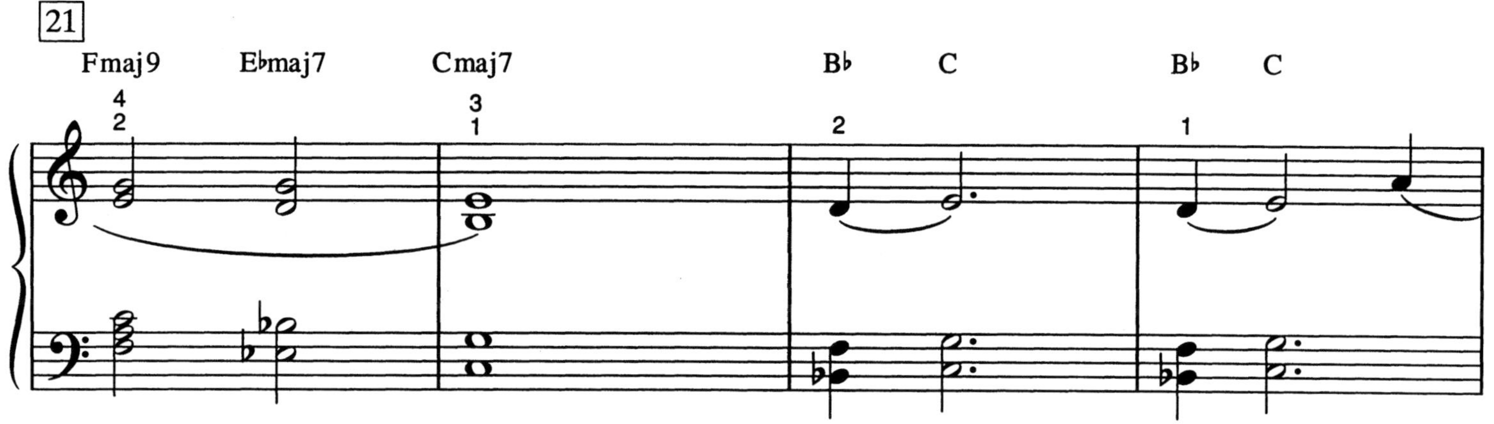
21 Fmaj9   Ebmaj7   Cmaj7   Bb   C   Bb   C

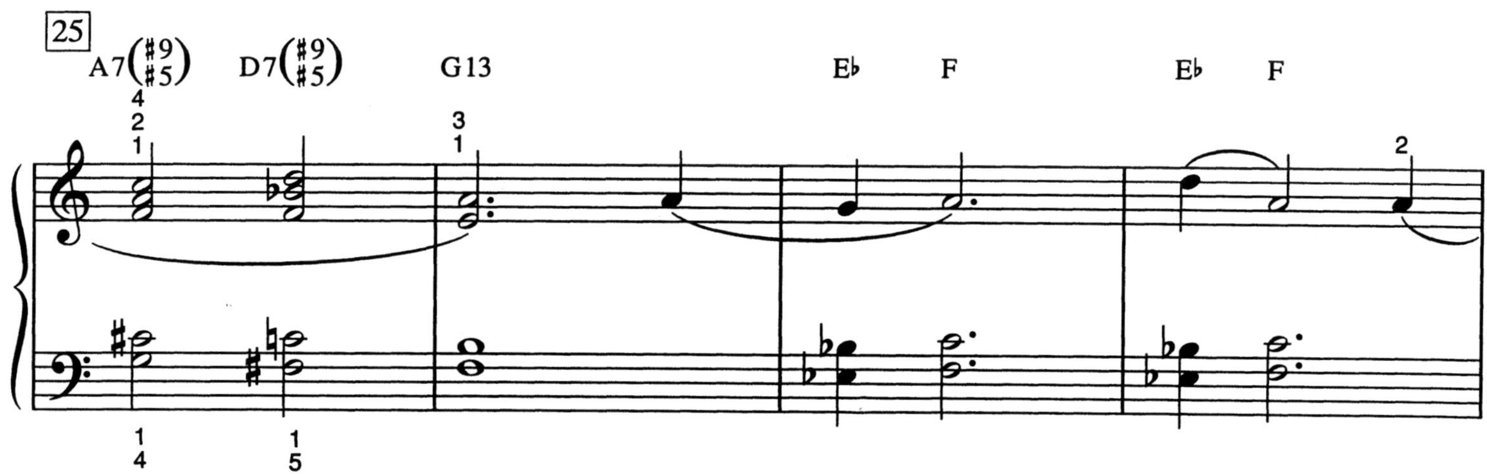
25 A7(#9)(#5)   D7(#9)(#5)   G13   Eb   F   Eb   F

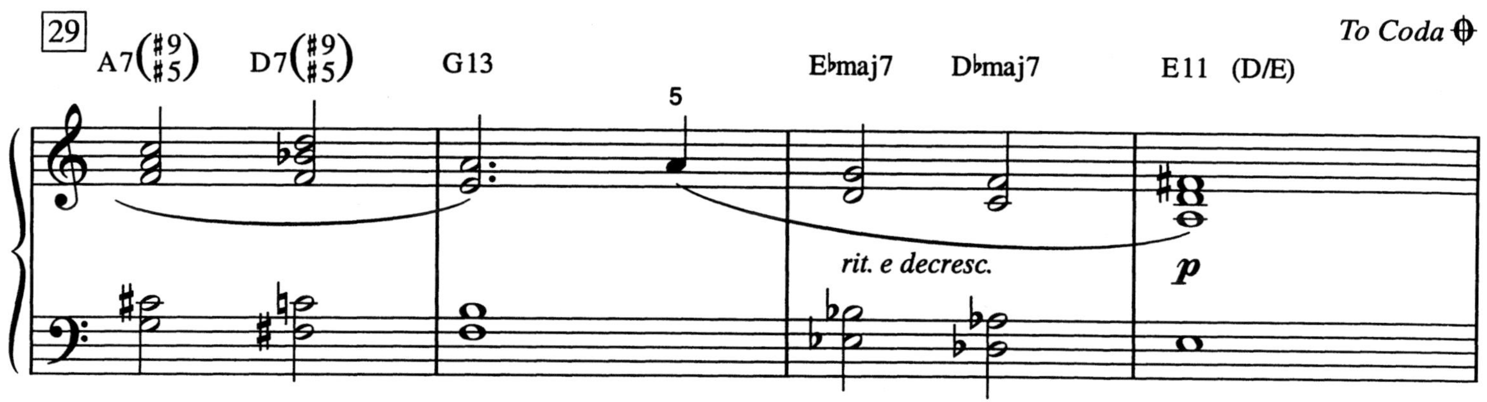
To Coda
29 A7(#9)(#5)   D7(#9)(#5)   G13   Ebmaj7   Dbmaj7   E11 (D/E)
rit. e decresc.
p

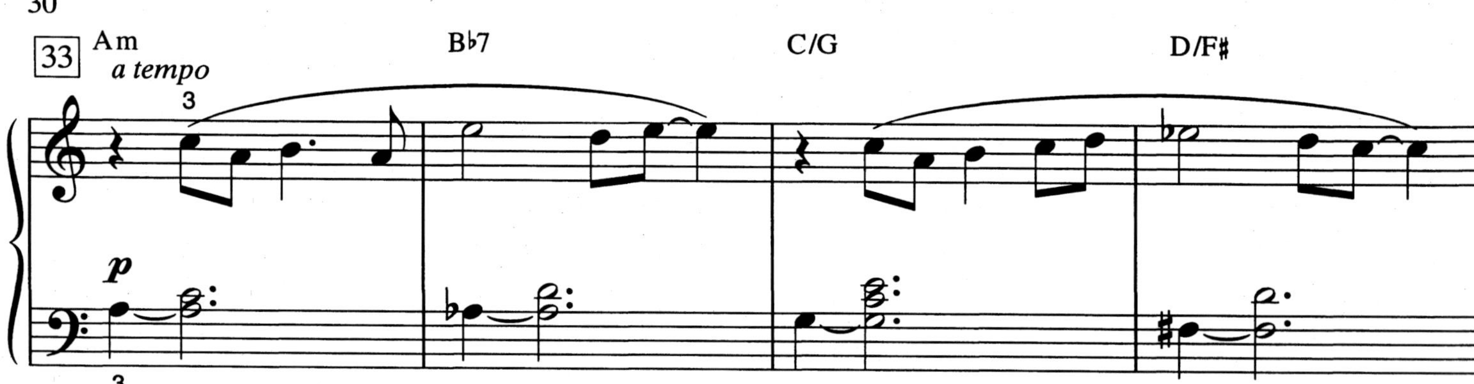
33
Am
a tempo
3
Bb7
C/G
D/F#
p
3
pedal simile

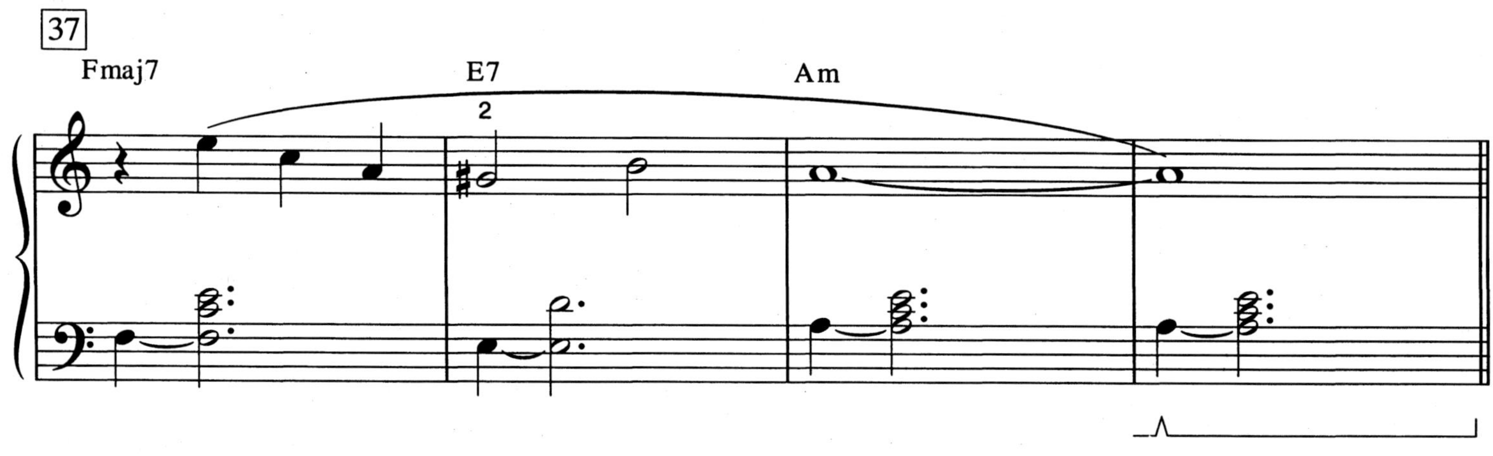
37
Fmaj7
E7
2
Am

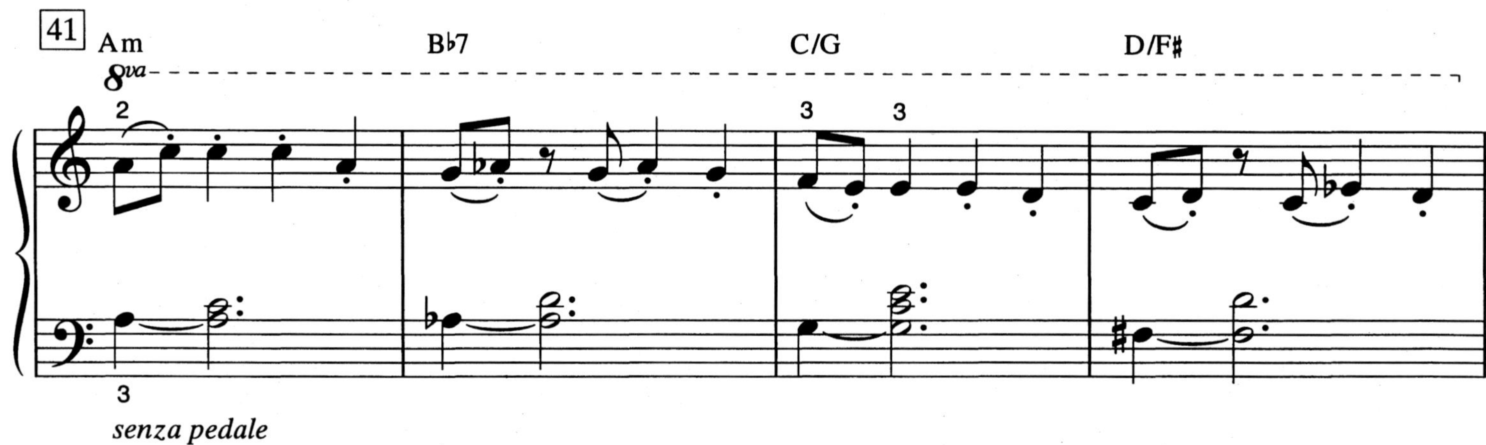
41
Am
8va
2
Bb7
C/G
3
3
D/F#
3
senza pedale

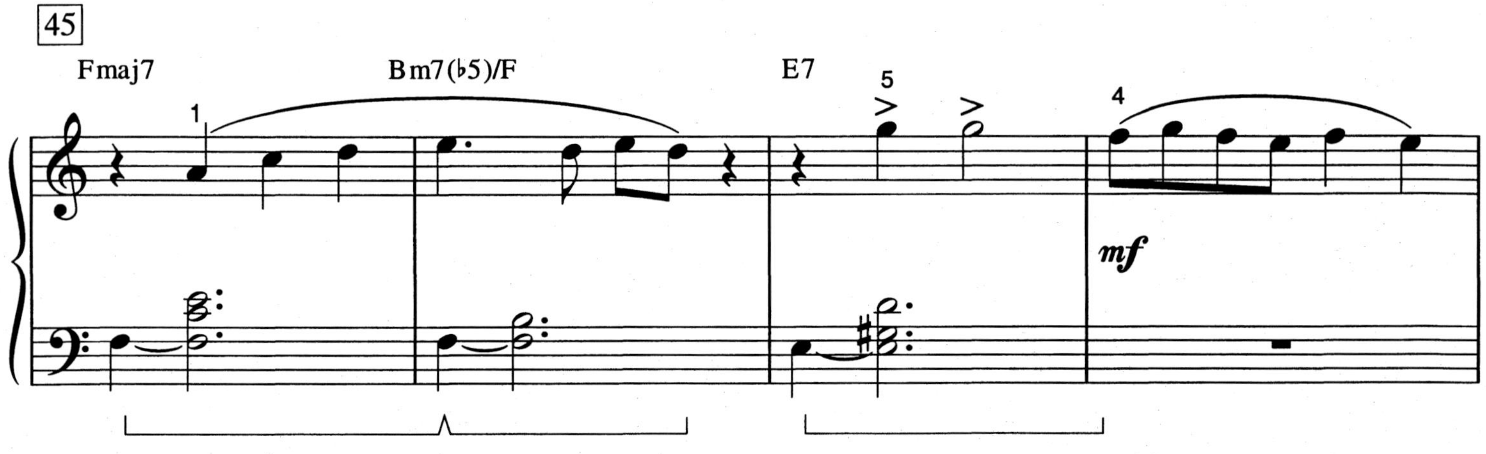
45
Fmaj7
1
Bm7(b5)/F
E7
5
4
mf

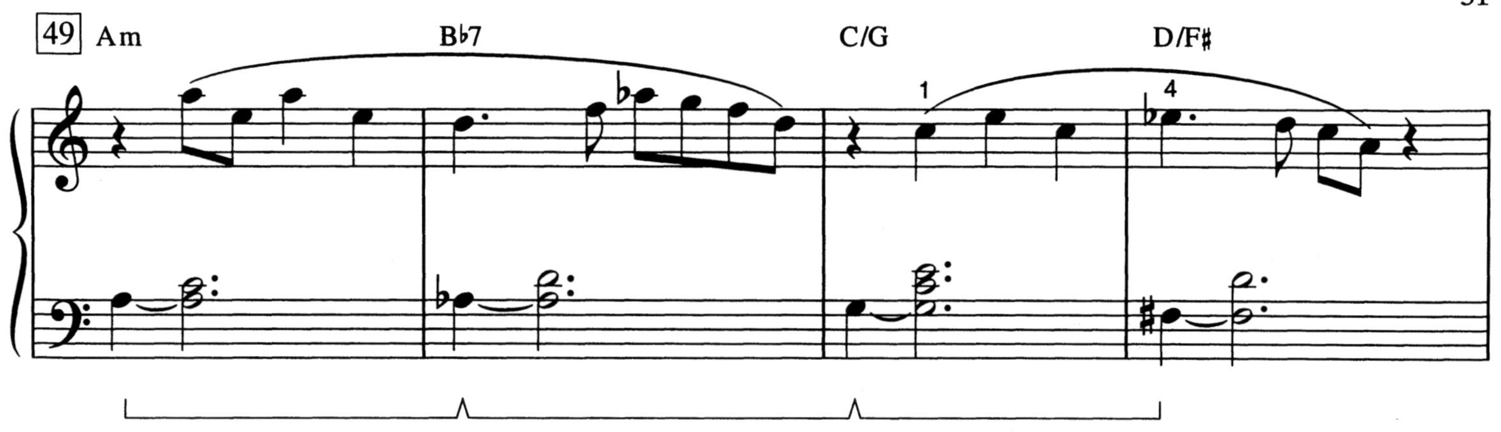

49 Am
B♭7
C/G
D/F♯

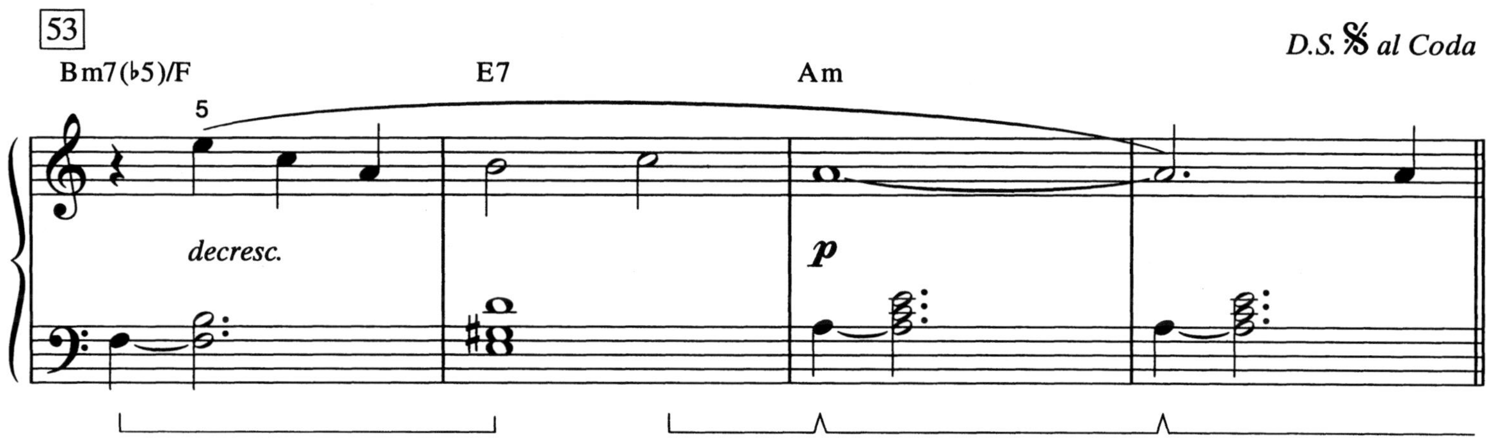

53
D.S. % al Coda
Bm7(♭5)/F
E7
Am
decresc.
p

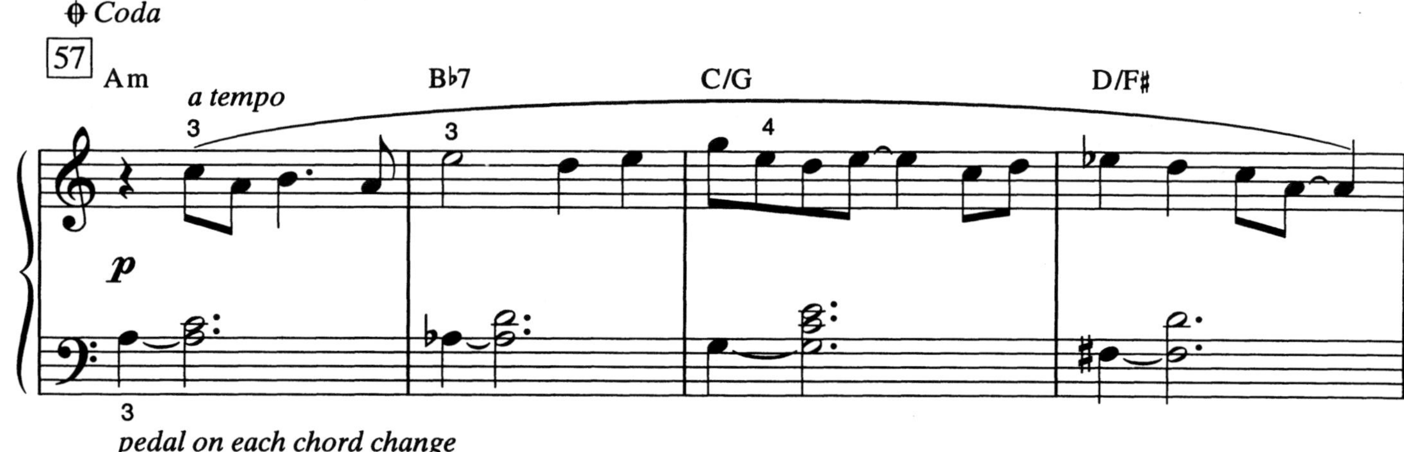

Coda
57 Am
a tempo
B♭7
C/G
D/F♯
p
pedal on each chord change

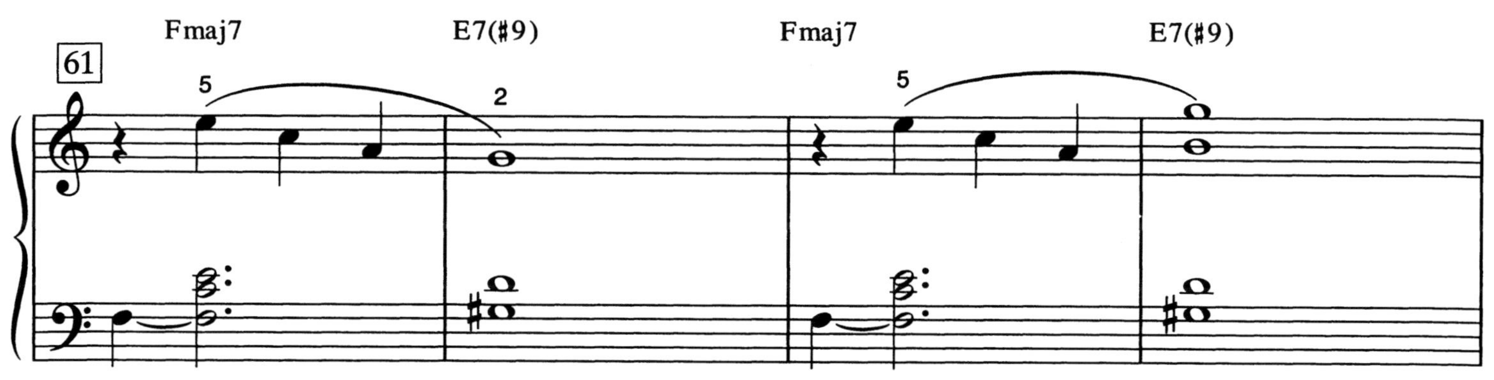

Fmaj7
E7(♯9)
Fmaj7
E7(♯9)
61

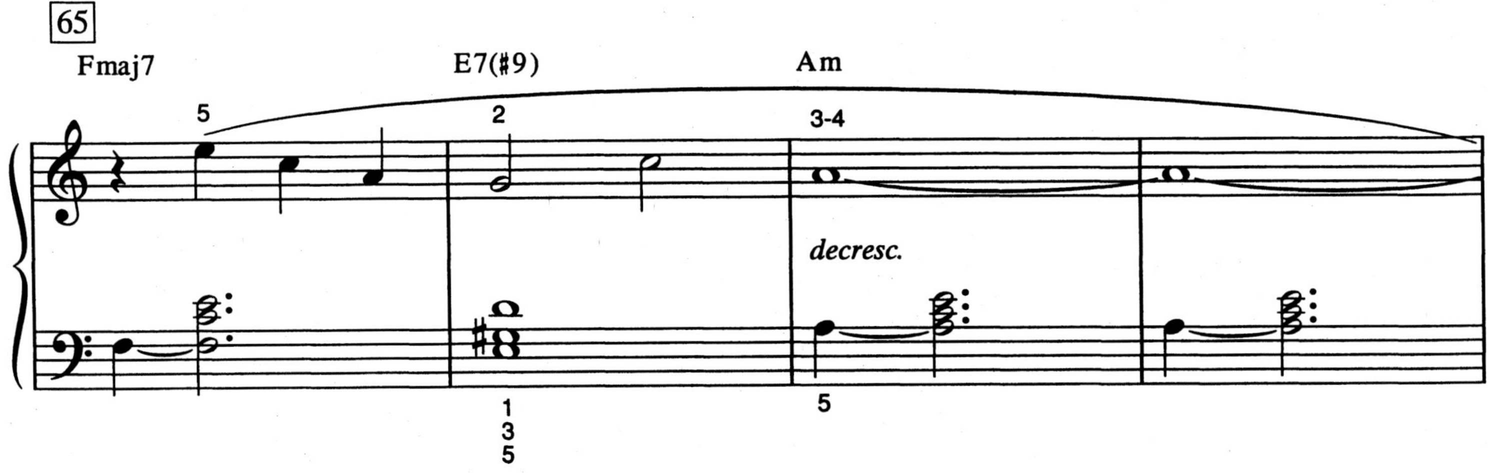

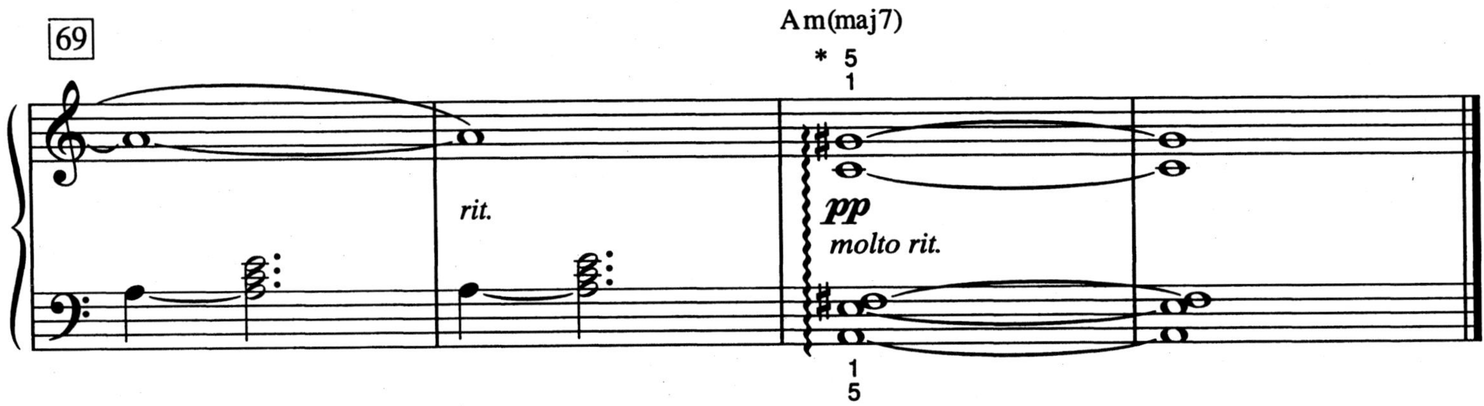

*Roll chord very slowly from the bottom note.